Gilfond, Henry
Heroines of America. N.Y., Fleet Press Corp., [c1970].
136 p. ports. 5.95

74-118207

heroines
of
america

Books in this Series

Heroes of Conservation
Heroes of Israel
Heroes of the American Indian
Heroes of Journalism
Heroes of Music
Heroines of America
Heroes of Mexico
Heroes of Science
Heroes of Puerto Rico
Heroes de Puerto Rico
    (Spanish language edition)
Heroes of Peace
Heroes of Nature

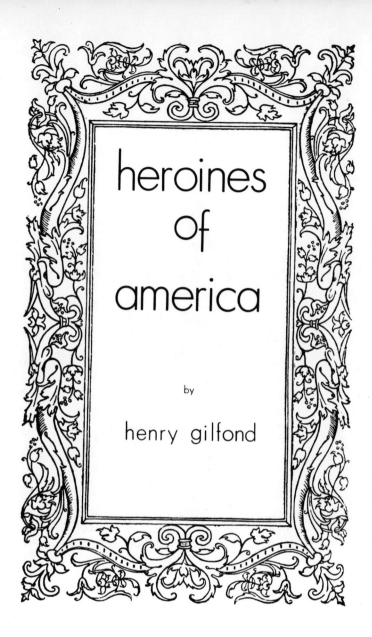

heroines
of
america

by

henry gilfond

FLEET PRESS CORPORATION

New York

CONTENTS

1	Heroines All	7
2	Jane Addams	10
3	Lillian D. Wald	17
4	Suffragettes	22
5	Elizabeth Blackwell	25
6	Clara Barton	32
7	Harriet Tubman	41
8	Sojourner Truth	49
9	Mary McLeod Bethune	53
10	Helen Keller	57
11	Margaret Sanger	64
12	Eleanor Roosevelt	70
13	Amelia Earhart	78
14	Mildred Didrickson Zaharias	86
15	Women in Washington	
	Margaret Chase Smith	91
	Shirley Chisholm	95
16	Heroines Without Sword	
	Writers	98
	Theatre	109
17	Marian Anderson	114
18	Georgia O'Keefe	119
19	Margaret Bourke-White	121
20	Maria Mitchell	124
21	Coretta King	128
	Index	135

HEROINES ALL

Bayard Taylor, an American poet, novelist, diplomat and world traveler of the last century, wrote:

"The brave are the tenderest,
The loving are daring."

He may have well written these lines in honor of the so many women whose courage and daring have brought honor to America, and indeed the world.

They were on the Mayflower, braving the storms of the Atlantic and the promise of a wilderness in their search for freedom. Women have always been in the forefront of the battle for freedom. They tilled the soil, helped build their homes, went hungry with their men, in the hard and often cruel first years in the New World.

They were a comfort to their children and an inspiration to

their husbands but, if need be, they could quarrel with their men, too, in their zeal for liberty.

Anne Hutchinson rebelled against the harsh rule of the Massachusetts Bay Colony, established her own colony in what was to become the state of Rhode Island. She would die, later in an Indian massacre, but not before her work was done. It was a woman, Anne Hutchinson, who struck the first blow for religious freedom in America.

Other women, many women, would give their lives to the building of democracy in our country. Almost all of them lived and died without fanfare, without the glories which they richly deserved. They are the women who moved westward, away from the comparatively safe Atlantic seaboard, through the Alleghenies, toward the Mississippi, and beyond. They lived in rude cabins, rode long miles on buckboard and in covered wagons. They suffered strange lands, cross weather and attacks by unfriendly Indians. They built a land, they bore children, they shouldered their guns at the sides of their husbands, and they died young.

They shouldered guns, too, in the War for American Independence. Molly Pitcher was one such woman. Margaret Corbin saw her husband felled by a Red-coat bullet; she picked up his musket and fought in his place.

There were other kinds of fighting, other kinds of battles in which America proved its heroines.

When John Zenger was jailed by the British in an effort to shut off his "rebellious" editorials, his wife, Anna Zenger, rose to publish as well as edit the New York *Weekly Journal.*

Women have never lagged in the struggle for freedom. Julia Ward Howe and Frances Wright were among the leaders in the battle to abolish slavery in the United States. Harriet Beecher Stowe's novel, *Uncle Tom's Cabin,* struck perhaps the greatest single anti-slavery blow in the country. Sojourner Truth and Harriet Tubman, women and ex-slaves, both, were truly heroic in the battle against slavery.

A democracy intends equal rights for all its citizens, but the women of America had to fight for those equal rights, and the heroines of this continuing struggle are many.

First there was the battle for suffrage, the right to vote. It may seem strange today, but it was not too long ago that women were not allowed to cast their ballots at the polls. It took the 19th Amendment to the Constitution of the United States, August 18th, 1920, to give women that elementary democratic right.

Jane Addams, Amelia Bloomer, Susan Anthony, Abigail Duniway were some of the brighter stars in this struggle for women's rights. But, as in the battle against the wilderness, many a heroine remains unsung and still to be honored.

There were other rights for which women have had to fight. Elizabeth Blackwell fought against great odds to become the first woman doctor in the United States. Margaret Chase Smith was the first American woman elected to our country's Senate. Anna Cora Mowatt made professional acting a respectable profession for women in America. Maria Mitchell was the first American woman to be recognized, internationally, as a great astronomer.

Nor did the women stop their battle with the winning of their own natural rights. Clara Barton organized the American Red Cross. Eleanor Roosevelt was honored as a spokesman for freedom and human rights. Rachel Carson lifted a great voice in fight against world pollution and for conservation. Daisy Bates was a force in the struggle for equal rights and equal opportunity for all of America's people, whatever their race, color or creed.

There is no end to the list of America's heroines. There is no phase or area of American life in which they have not given, and continue to give all of their energies, their love and their blood.

Some of these women have written their names large in the history of our country. So many more whose names will never be known, each in her own way, in some measure, has added to the story of the heroism of America's women.

This book will attempt to throw some light on the history of some of the brighter stars in this galaxy of heroines, on the shape of their lives, on their dreams, and on their great accomplishments.

JANE ADDAMS
THEY CALLED HER "SAINT JANE"

She was born with a curvature of the spine, her back was bent and crooked, she walked pigeon-toed, her head drooped to one side; but so great was her inner-beauty that she was perhaps the most loved woman of her time.

Jane Addams was born in Cedarville, Illinois, September 6th, 1860. She would not remember her mother who died when Jane was still an infant. She would always be aware of her father, however. John Addams was a wealthy mill owner, a banker, a state senator, a friend of Abraham Lincoln, and a strikingly handsome man. He was so handsome that Jane would quietly move away from him whenever they were together in public places. She was a sensitive child. She was sensitive to all her deformity. Fortunately, for herself, for America, for the world, she was sensitive to much more, and of greater importance than her body.

Her father helped. He explained why he wept, when Abraham Lincoln was assassinated. He explained why he sorrowed for the death of Giuseppe Mazzini, the great Italian patriot and soldier for freedom. He devoted hours to discussing with his daughter the importance of righteous thinking and righteous action. But it was Jane, herself, and at the very early age of seven, who put to her father the question which was to occupy the greater part of her life.

She was riding with her father through the mill-town section of Cedarville. This was the part of town in which the poor people lived.

"Why do people live in such horrid little houses?" asked Jane. "And why are the houses so close together?"

John Addams explained, as best he could, to the young child. There were economic factors. The poor could not buy large tracts of land. The poor could not afford the cost of large houses. Nor did John Addams neglect the morality of the situation. Poverty was an evil and, like all evils, it should be erased.

How much of her father's explanation the seven year old Jane Addams understood would be difficult to estimate. Her reaction to the talk, however, was immediate and prophetic.

"I'm going to have a big house, when I grow up," she said.

"Of course," said her father.

"But I won't build it where there are other big houses," continued the child. "I'll build it among all these little houses, all the horrid little houses like these."

And she would. The impressions of childhood often direct the course of one's life. This was particularly true of Jane Addams.

At the age of seventeen, Jane was enrolled in the Rockford Seminary in Illinois. She majored in Greek, history and mathematics but, very early, she determined to study medicine.

"I'm going to become a doctor and live and work among the poor," she said.

She enrolled in the Philadelphia Women's Medical College at the age of 21. Jane was a determined young woman. She had

Jane Addams

set herself a goal, and she meant to achieve that goal. She would be a doctor for the poor.

Unfortunately, sometimes the strongest desire, the greatest will, is not enough to carry us to a successful conclusion, a mission accomplished. Jane Addams entered the Philadelphia Women's Medical College in the fall of 1881, as she had planned, but even before she could complete her first year at the school, her proposed medical career came to an abrupt halt.

The curvature of the spine, which had always been a problem to her, suddenly became a most serious disorder. She tried to struggle against the inordinate pains she suffered, and did; but when the pains became so violent that she could not attend classes or read a book, Jane had to look for help.

She was sent to a hospital and it was six months before she was allowed to walk again. Even then, she was cautioned to limit her activities and to keep clear of any physical, emotional, even intellectual involvement.

The doctors also advised her to go to Europe for a couple of years, just to rest.

Jane Addams was already too involved to follow the prescription of her doctors to the letter. She did go to Europe for two years. Her medical career was over before it had been actually started. But her mind would not rest, nor would her need to do something for the poor be diminished.

When she was in the hospital, Jane could do little more than read and think. Even in Europe, her physical movement limited, she could do very little. The need to leave medical school had come as a great disappointment. She had promised herself that she would become a doctor for the poor. She could not keep that promise. But, gradually, reading and thinking, she began to realize that "there were other reasons for living among the poor and practicing medicine upon them."

At first her ideas were vague, ideas which came out of the books she read. Those ideas would take shape and mature when Jane Addams decided that it wasn't enough to read about life, that she must live it.

She walked in the slums of London in England, the slums of

Berlin in Germany, the slums of Madrid in Spain, the slums of Rome in Italy.

"I was irresistibly drawn to the poorer quarters of each city," she wrote.

She attended the meetings of the "Match Girls," when those poor sellers of matches went on strike. She watched as the poor bid for rotten fruit and vegetables in the market auctions. She noted the drab clothes of the laboring men and the gnarled fingers of women who were still young. And she was horrified by it. Perhaps she was even more horrified by her inability to do anything about it.

"I'm a wealthy, privileged bus-top spectator of poverty," she said.

It was a posture she didn't like. That posture was going to change.

Jane had been traveling with an old school-mate, Ellen Starr. She suggested that they visit Toynbee Hall in London. Toynbee Hall was a settlement house where people came to settle and work among the poor, to help the poor while living with them.

The two young women were deeply impressed with what they saw. Here was theory put to practice. People were not just talking about poverty, they were doing something about it. Suddenly there was light and direction for the work Jane Addams had always intended. She would no longer be a witness of the poor and their deprivations; she would act against it.

Jane Addams was 29 years old at the time and the pains of her spinal deformity would never leave her, but at long last she knew she was about to deliver on that promise she had made when she was a young girl; she was going to build herself that big house among all those little, horrid crowded houses.

They found the house in Chicago, at 335 South Halsted Street. The house had once been used by the Little Sisters of the Poor as a home for the aged, but it had been neglected and had become nothing more than an eye-sore. There was a saloon on one side of the building, a funeral home on the other. Its neighbors were Irish, Italian, German, Greek, Russian, Polish, a melting pot of European immigrants, living in squalor. The street was unpaved and uncollected garbage was strewed about.

It was hardly a street or a building to inspire great works, but Jane Addams was determined in her efforts. The future Hull House was a respectably cleaned and polished house when Jane and Ellen Starr moved in.

Needed help came quickly. Helen Culver, the owner of the building, deeply moved by Jane's program, refused to take any rent for the house. Women from wealthier neighborhoods came to organize classes and teach sewing, cooking, dressmaking and millinery. There were clubs for the boys and the girls. There was a nursery where working mothers could leave their children for five cents a day; the fee included lunch for the children.

At first the neighborhood was a little suspicious.

"What's in it for them?"

But the suspicion gave way to affection as Jane Addams kept expanding her program.

There were classes in child care, dancing, dramatics and music. There was a gym for the older children and men, a playground for the young. There were concerts and dramatic presentations and even an Old Settler's Party for the older residents of the neighborhood.

Hull House was established. It grew.

There was a Jane Club providing cooperative housing for working girls. There was the Working People's Social Science Club. There was an organization for the cooperative purchasing of coal. There was a music school.

Hull House was a great success, but Jane Addams never let herself dream of success. Her task was to combat poverty and all its evils. Hull House was just the beginning of her program, just the very beginning of her life-long work.

She fought for child labor laws, when the youngest of children were working in the sweat shops. She campaigned for safety laws in the factories where countless men and women were being maimed for the lack of safety provisions. She battled for adult education, for day nurseries, for city sanitary codes. She argued, made speeches for a State Board of Conciliation and Arbitration to cut down the suffering of working people due to long and endless strikes. She was instrumental, as she was in all her campaigns for reform, in establishing state controlled, free employment bureaus.

There was no end to the energies of this inspired woman.

She labored for woman suffrage. She toiled for better housing, for public baths, for a law controlling the sale of drugs. She was a member of the Chicago Board of Education and President of the National Conference of Charities and Correction.

Theodore Roosevelt called her "America's most useful citizen."

She was a member of the Executive Committee of the American Union Against Militarism and chairman of the Women's Peace Party. She was the chairman of the International Committee of Women for Permanent Peace and President of the International Congress of Women.

Walter Lippmann, one of America's most respected political thinkers and writers, spoke of Jane Addams as a "cathedral of compassion."

Her work and her worth did not go unnoticed. Yale University bestowed the master's degree on her. It was the first honorary degree Yale had ever given a woman. The Congress of Social Workers called her the "First Citizen of Chicago, America, and the World." In 1931, she was awarded the Nobel Peace Prize. But, more important than all these degrees and titles to Jane Addams, was the manner in which settlement houses sprung up and grew around the country. Each settlement house added to the glory of the works of Jane Addams.

John Burns, a leader of British labor, said of her, "She was the only saint America has produced."

The *New York Times,* in an editorial, declared of Jane Addams, "(she was) a social statesman of saintly statesmanship."

The day she was notified that she and Dr. Nicholas Murray Butler were to share the 1931 Nobel Peace Award, she entered Johns Hopkins Hospital in Baltimore for the second in a series of operations. On May 21st, 1935, at the age of 75, the "saint" died.

The "saint" died, but the work she began will never cease; nor will the honor to her name.

LILLIAN D. WALD
ANGEL AMONG THE PUSHCARTS

Like Jane Addams, Lillian Wald came from a cultured and well-to-do family. Like Jane Addams, Lillian Wald had the desire and need to live and work among the poor. Like Jane Addams, Lillian Wald left a name and a tradition to be remembered.

She was born in Cincinnati, Ohio, on March 10th, 1867, but lived most of her childhood and her youth in Rochester, New York. Her father, Max D. Wald, was a dealer in optical wares. Her grandfather, Goodman Schwarz, had come to this country from Germany in the migration which followed the rebellion and defeat of the freedom fighters of 1848. The love of liberty, an awareness of injustice, the crusading spirit, were all part and parcel of Lillian D. Wald's inheritance.

In 1889, at the age of 22, she came to New York and enrolled in the New York Hospital School for Nursing. She was graduated in 1891 and, in the fall of that year, she was a nurse in the New York Juvenile Asylum.

As a probationer in the hospital, Lillian had gotten into difficulties because she rebelled against the stiff discipline. Most often her bouts with the authorities came about because of her need to give that extra bit of attention to some poor sick man or woman. In the Juvenile Hospital, she resented the mechanical and brutal way in which the poor children were treated. She tried to bring about changes but the hospital authorities were not to be moved. Lillian Wald, however, would not be stopped. She would find a way to help.

She entered Women's Medical College of New York in 1892. As a doctor, she would have more authority to deal with the ills she saw than she had had as a nurse. But, again like Jane Addams, she would never get her degree in medicine. The course of her life had other adventures in store for her.

As a student in the medical school, Lillian was asked to teach a class in home nursing in the lower east side of New York. The lower east side today, except for some public and cooperative construction, teems with poverty. In 1893, there was nothing but teeming poverty.

It was an area of the city in which thousands upon thousands of immigrants were jammed into old and broken-down houses. There were no baths and very little plumbing. The streets were thick with peddlers, pushcarts and garbage. While most of the immigrants had come to the New World for freedom and a better life, this was a place which bred gangsters and violence.

Lillian Wald had seen poverty in the New York Hospital and in the Juvenile Asylum, but nothing like she witnessed on the lower east side. She was shocked, but not frightened. She plunged into her work with an eager determination and, from the beginning, she had nothing but love and compassion for her less fortunate students.

One morning, at the end of her home nursing class, a youngster approached her, timidly.

"My mother is sick."

Lillian took the child's hand, and the child led her up the

18

Lillian Wald

rotting stairs of an old tenement house, and into the miserable rooms in which she lived. For the next hours, and well into the night, Lillian Wald tended the child's mother. She washed and bathed her. She changed the sheets of her bed and mopped the dirty floors. Lillian was doing only what she felt she needed to do, but the gratitude in the eyes of the sick mother and the children suddenly opened the young Lillian's eyes to the purpose for which she had been reaching.

The very next morning she made a call on Mrs. Solomon Loeb, an elderly and wealthy woman who gave much to charity and worthy causes. She outlined a plan that had kept her awake all night. There was poverty on the lower east side, ignorance and disease. It needed nurses, trained nurses, to live among the poor and to work with them.

Mrs. Loeb was impressed. She enlisted the aid of her son-in-law, Jacob Schiff. Together, they offered Lillian a program. They would provide sufficient funds to pay each nurse $60 a month to cover the living expenses. They would also provide a fund for medicines and food for the sick and the poor. It was a generous offer and Lillian accepted it eagerly.

With Mary Brewster, a friend and a nurse, she moved into the College Settlement, one of the first settlement houses in the country, and started her work immediately. It wasn't easy. There were so many poor, and so many ill. The need for funds for food and drugs kept growing. There was need for more and more nurses, too.

But Lillian Wald was equal to the task. She got up the facts and the figures. She pleaded her cause wherever she went. She urged people to contribute what they could; and people gave.

Within two years, Lillian had collected enough contributions to move into better and larger quarters, and to gather around her a solid corps of registered Visiting Nurses. These quarters were located at 265 Henry Street, a three-story brick house which still operates as a community center for the lower east side.

One can do much in such a solid little building, and Lillian Wald did it. Once the nursing program was functioning well enough to please her, she began to organize a number of classes, in reading, cooking, and citizenship. She organized clubs for the young people as well. There were classes in art, music, dancing, and theatre. Irving Berlin, George Gershwin and Eddie Cantor were among the young boys who came to Henry Street Settlement and later went on to fame and fortune.

But Lillian Wald, again like Jane Addams, could not rest with one great accomplishment. She helped create the Outdoor Recreation League, whose purpose was to provide open playgrounds for the young people of the city. She fought for school doctors and nurses, and New York City was the first to have a trained nurse in every one of its schools.

And she fought for child labor laws, for factory safety laws, and for better housing for the poor, until her death in 1940.

Today there are two memorials in honor of her work. There are the Lillian D. Wald houses, a low rental housing project on the lower east side of New York, and a plaque in her honor in the Henry Street Playground. But there are other memorials, memorials without name, the young men and women whose prominence in civic life had its beginnings in the Henry Street Settlement House and in all those other settlement houses which were established and grew under the influence of this heroic woman, Lillian D. Wald.

4

SUFFRAGETTES

On July 19, 1848, at Seneca Falls in New York, Elizabeth Cady Stanton, Lucretia Mott, and a number of other brave women, issued what amounted to a declaration of war. They demanded that America grant its women the right to vote. They gave notice to the country at large that they were ready and willing to fight for that right.

Elizabeth Cady Stanton (1815-1902), daughter of a judge and wife of a leading anti-slavery journalist, was a brilliant woman, a great speaker, and an equally magnificent writer. She fought not only for the women's rights at the polls; she devoted her entire life to the struggle for all the rights which properly belong to women, legal and industrial, as well as political. She did not live to see her goals achieved but, as we know, she did not work in vain.

Susan B. Anthony

Elizabeth C. Stanton

Lucretia Mott (1793-1880) fought for the rights of labor, for peace, and against slavery, as well as for the rights of women. She organized the Female Anti-Slavery Society. Her home was a station on the Underground Railroad, that railroad whose trains carried so many slaves fleeing their masters, to the North and freedom.

Susan B. Anthony (1820-1906) is probably the best known name in the fight for woman's suffrage. With Elizabeth Cady Stanton, she organized the National Woman Suffrage Association. She was president of the National American Woman Suffrage Association. She led groups of women to the polls, to test the women's right to vote. She was arrested, tried by jury and fined, but it took a Supreme Court decision, against her, to stop her attacks at the polls.

As with other suffragettes, Miss Anthony's work did not end with her struggle for suffrage. She was one of the organizers in 1863 of the Women's Loyal League to support Abraham Lincoln's battle to free the slaves. She got the State of New York to pass laws which guaranteed women the control of their own property and the right to keep the wages they earned, wherever they worked.

Julia Ward Howe (1819-1910), famous for writing "The Battle Hymn of the Republic," fought against slavery and for peace as hard as she fought for the right to vote. It is interesting to note, too, that she was the first woman elected to the American Academy of Arts and Letters.

They were all heroines, but attaining the right to vote was only one of the many and continuing victories of women in their wars for equality. There were other areas, and there remain other areas, in which women must struggle for their rights. Where victories have been achieved, there are heroines; where victories have yet to be achieved, there will be other heroines.

5

ELIZABETH BLACKWELL, M. D.

There are many women who are doctors today, many women working in every important branch of medicine. Perhaps there are not as many as there might be; there is a shortage of doctors of medicine in every part of the world. But, there was a time, and not too very long ago, when it was unthinkable that a woman might become a doctor in the United States. It was Elizabeth Blackwell, who through some mighty heroic action, brought that situation and prejudice to an end.

Her father, Samuel Blackwell, was a sugar refiner, and his business was located in Bristol, England. His thinking was advanced for his time. He was opposed to slavery and to child labor. He was a firm believer in equal education and opportunity for women. His beliefs and his speeches didn't help his business, but they left their good impression on his children.

In 1832, his business failing, Samuel Blackwell and his nine children left Bristol for a growing and busy New York in the still very young United States. Six years later, he took his family to the still younger Cincinnati, Ohio. There, unhappily, at a very early age, Samuel Blackwell died, leaving nothing but poverty and his love of freedom to his children.

Elizabeth had been born in 1821 and was only seventeen when her father died. She had adored her father, and the loss was great, but there was little time for mourning. There was a family of younger brothers and sisters to feed, clothe, and house.

First, together with two of the older Blackwell sisters, Elizabeth organized and opened a day and boarding school. It didn't do too well and had to be closed. Elizabeth found a job teaching in the small town of Henderson, Kentucky.

It wasn't a very good job. The people of Henderson seemed to be making no more than a gesture, furnishing a school for its children. Certainly, they did nothing to make the teaching of the eager young Elizabeth Blackwell easier, or even welcome. On the contrary, they seemed to do everything possible to make the teaching of their children an impossibility.

The young Elizabeth might have been easily discouraged; she wasn't.

She had the schoolhouse cleaned up, the floor and the walls and the ceiling repaired. She started with twenty-one pupils, but, soon, there were more students than the room could hold.

"I teach ten hours, three days of the week," Elizabeth wrote back to Cincinnati, "and wish the other three were similarly filled."

It was a heavy teaching load, but young Elizabeth was equal to it. Elizabeth Blackwell never shirked work. It was the circumstance around that work which troubled her, and troubled her deeply.

"I suppose that I see slavery here," she wrote, "in its milder form."

She never saw a slave whipped or treated with the extreme cruelty so common at that time. Still she rebelled against the sight of "beings drudging on from earliest morning to latest night, cuffed about by everyone, scolded all day long, blamed

26

unjustly."

"It is dreadful to live among them," she wrote, "utterly unable to help them."

She completed her year's work in Henderson and left her post in that slave-ridden state. The anti-slavery sentiments of her father, Samuel Blackwell, left their mark on his children. They would all become involved, one way or another, in the abolitionist movement to free the slaves in America.

It was during the summer following her experience in Henderson that Elizabeth Blackwell suddenly became aware of the ambition which was to dominate the rest of her life.

"If only there were a lady doctor," said her ailing friend, Mary Donaldson, "how much less would I need to suffer."

Lady doctor? There were no lady doctors. Why not?

Her father would have called the situation preposterous and would have said that a woman had the right to become anything she wished, doctor, lawyer, president of the United States.

Elizabeth Blackwell knew well enough how much the odds were stacked against her, but odds would never interfere with her will or her determination. She was her father's daughter. Once the idea was born, once she had mulled it over, once she had come to a decision, nothing would stop her.

"Where will you get the money? You need money to go to school. You need money for food and lodging, for clothes, for books."

"I'll work for the money. I'll save it for school."

"And what medical school will admit you? What medical school will accept a woman?"

"I'll meet that problem in due time."

Immediately, she began to investigate the job possibilities. She wanted a teaching job which would also give her the opportunity to study, to study medicine. And luck, for once, was with her.

Dr. John Dickson was the head of a school in Asheville, North Carolina. He needed a music teacher for his school, and Elizabeth applied for the job. She applied with a condition. She would teach music in Dr. Dickson's school if he permitted her the use of his personal medical library.

The doctor may have been amused by the condition Miss Blackwell presented. He may have beeen irritated by this young woman's demands. But he needed a music teacher. Elizabeth Blackwell got the job, and for the next six years she taught music in Asheville, and studied in the medical library of Dr. Dickson.

Six years of studying medical books, however, do not make a doctor or give one the right to practice medicine. Elizabeth needed to enroll in a medical school and get her degree before she could call herself a physician. In the summer of 1847, when Elizabeth Blackwell made her first thrust in this direction, women in medical schools were completely unknown. No woman in the United States, at that time, was a doctor or had ever been admitted into a medical college.

Dr. Warrington, an old friend of the Blackwell family, shook his head when Elizabeth came to him in Philadelphia. Philadelphia was the medical center of America in those days, but Dr. Warrington didn't think it was ready for women students.

"Nursing, perhaps," the doctor suggested.

It was Elizabeth's turn to shake her head.

"I want to become a physician. I will become a physician."

Dr. Warrington was kind and gentle. He did what he could for the young lady. She was permitted to attend his lectures, read in his library, but he was helpless when it came to her actual enrollment in a medical college.

At one time the good doctor suggested, perhaps only half-seriously, that Elizabeth get dressed in a man's clothing and pretend to be a man.

Elizabeth wasn't offended. She knew the doctor meant well. But the idea was completely unacceptable to her. For Elizabeth Blackwell, it was as important to break the barriers against equal rights for women, as it was to become the first woman physician.

She tried at every medical school in Philadelphia. She tried the College of Physicians and Surgeons in New York. She applied for admission to Harvard, Bowdoin, Geneva. They all turned her down, except one. That one was Geneva Medical College, the school which later was to change its name to Hobart. Elizabeth Blackwell was on her way.

The young lady medical student was something of a curiosity in Geneva. It took the male students a little while to grow accustomed to a female among them. It took a while longer before they dropped the "Miss" from her name and just called her "Blackwell." But they were never unfriendly.

The town's people, on the other hand, were hostile when Elizabeth first arrived. A woman who didn't get married, didn't stay home, have children and wash and cook, was considered a little odd, and more often than not, indecent. It took them a longer time to accept the young female medical student; but they finally did. When Elizabeth Blackwell was graduated from Geneva with a degree in medicine, the women of the town came to attend, not with curiosity or antagonism, but to applaud and to cheer this courageous young woman.

Elizabeth Blackwell had made a giant step in her career and in the struggle for equal rights for women. But the young doctor was not prepared to practice. She felt that her medical education wasn't sufficiently thorough. She wanted to became a surgeon, as well as a physician. She sailed for Paris where she hoped to complete her training for her profession.

But Paris was no more liberal in its views of women's rights than was the United States. Doctor's degree and all, Elizabeth Blackwell found the doors of the French medical schools closed to her. The situation for Dr. Blackwell was the same wherever she went in Europe. Polite receptions and polite refusals were the order of the day, still, Elizabeth would not give up her quest.

Elizabeth was going to continue her studies in Europe one way or another. She applied for the position of apprentice nurse at La Maternite, a women's hospital in Paris. Even as a nursing apprentice, she could observe the work of the French doctors, though it meant doing much menial work such as scrubbing floors and washing bed sheets. Elizabeth, always the determined young woman, never allowed pride to get in the way of her goal.

Unfortunately, it was an accident, the catching of an infectious disease, which cost her the loss of an eye and cut short her studies of medicine in Europe.

The loss of an eye is a frightening experience. It might have been enough to stop any ordinary person, whatever his endeavor, but Elizabeth Blackwell was not an ordinary person.

Back in New York, in 1851, she began to hunt for a suitable office for her practice. Again she met with closed doors, and even hostility. Landlords did not look with kindness or respect on professional women.

At long last, she found herself an office on University Place, near Washington Square and Greenwich Village, in New York. But she was not allowed to hang out a shingle, a sign with her name, nor did the patients come flocking to see her. On the contrary, there were no patients. It wasn't until she gave a series of classes in "Physical Education of Girls" that anyone came to her office. And it was one of her students who, finally, became her first patient.

But one patient, half a dozen patients, was not enough. There had to be another way. With her sister, Emily Blackwell, who had become a doctor, too, Elizabeth organized the New York Infirmary for Women and Children on Bleecker Street, in Greenwich Village. It was slow getting started. There were only 300 patients in its first year. But the opposition with which the hospital was greeted waned and, in its second year, Dr. Blackwell's hospital serviced 3,000 women and children. The achievement was significant. Dr. Blackwell was at last accepted as a full-fledged and capable physician. Women doctors had become respectable, even desirable. The New York Infirmary for Women and Children had to find larger quarters and moved to Second Avenue, with more floors, more rooms, and more facilities.

A few years later, Elizabeth Blackwell extended the work of her hospital. She urged the New York State legislature to establish a medical school for women. She had much support. The work of her hospital was enough to convince the New York lawmakers. The New York Women's Medical College opened its doors in 1866, just one year after the end of the Civil War, and Elizabeth was a member of its faculty.

One might think that Elizabeth Blackwell had done enough, had won enough victories in the continuing war for women's rights. One might think she had earned herself a rest, a little time to enjoy the fruits of her labors. One might think so, but not Dr. Blackwell.

England was without a women's medical school. England was without a women's hospital. England was the scene of her next battles, and her next victories.

It was in England that Elizabeth Blackwell died, in 1910, at the age of 89. She had led a full and heroic life. Today, there is an Elizabeth Blackwell House in Geneva, a Blackwell Medical School in Rochester, and a portrait of the great woman hangs on the walls of the London School of Medicine for Women, the school which she had helped to establish, and where she taught gynecology.

Truly, Elizabeth Blackwell, is one of America's great heroines.

Elizabeth Blackwell

6

CLARA BARTON
THE CALL TO MERCY

Clara Barton was the fifth and youngest child of her New England family. She was born on the 25th of December, Christmas, 1821, in the small town of Oxford, Massachusetts, a day of considerable significance to her pious parents. The Bartons were a religious family, and the Puritan strain was strong in them. Clara, for example, was never allowed so frivolous a toy as a doll, but there was love enough in her household to compensate for whatever else she lacked as a child. Love and mercy, were to prove the two keynotes in the life and work of Clara Barton.

She was a small child, not particularly strong. She was carefully cared for and protected by her mother and father, and her four older brothers and sisters, and perhaps that is why she was so shy, bashful, among strangers. Clara Barton would always have to struggle against her physical weaknesses. Her family would help her overcome her shyness.

In the beginning, on the Barton farm, Clara's playmates were the animal pets of the household, and her brother David. It was from David, a wild young man on a horse, that she learned how to ride. It was David, too, who gave Clara the knowledge of what she would do with her life.

They called the young man "Buffalo Bill" because of the way he stunted on his horse. Well, Buffalo Bill stunted once too often. He was thrown and badly hurt. For two years he was confined to his bed. During those two years, Clara Barton was his nurse.

She was constantly at his bedside. She forgot the outdoors. She forgot the horse-riding. The mission of her young years was to nurse her brother David back to health.

David eventually recovered, returned to his wild ways with a horse. But Clara had paled, grown thin, nervous, and was shyer than ever with strangers.

Her father sent her to a boarding school, hoping that absence from home would be a cure for the child's restraint with strangers. The plan didn't work. There were 150 girls at the boarding school. Clara Barton was the most miserable amongst them. Her education had to come closer to home.

First it was her brother Stephen and her sister Sally who were her teachers. Then it was the local school. Gradually, slowly, but surely, Clara emerged from the shell in which she had enclosed herself. It was Clara, herself, who finally realized that the full cure for her shyness, her timidity, would come only with her leaving the shelter of her home. Like a young bird, she must leave the nest, if she is to learn how to fly alone.

Her brother Stephen managed a mill. She asked him for a job at a spinning loom. It was her first adventure into the outside world, and things went well for Clara until there was a fire and the mill burned down to the ground. What now?

There was precious little a young girl could do on her own in the early 1800s. She got married and had children, or she taught school. Clara Barton chose to teach. At the age of 15, Clara established a school for the children of the factory workers in North Oxford.

Clara Barton

She taught for ten years, then moved on to Hightstown in New Jersey. Here she started a school with just six students, but, by the end of the year, the six had become six hundred. Clara's shyness and timidity were gone. She would never again be afraid to go out and meet people, mingle with strangers. She would never again be alone.

Her health was another matter. Clara Barton had worked hard in Hightstown and had given all her energies to the building of that school in New Jersey. Her efforts took their toll. She had become frail, weak; she could hardly use her voice at all. Unhappily, Clara Barton could no longer teach. After eighteen years in the classroom, the young woman had to look elsewhere for her career, a career which would demand less of her energies, and little of her throat.

She had helped her brother Stephen with his bookkeeping, when Stephen managed the mill in Massachusetts. She knew she could be useful, even valuable, working in an office. There were many offices in Washington, D.C. and this would be the logical place to look for the kind of job she wanted. The trouble was, while there were many offices and many clerks in the capital, the government had never employed a woman.

"There always must be a first one," said Clara, and the once shy young woman was able to convince her congressman from Massachusetts.

Clara Barton was appointed to a position in the Department of the Interior, the first woman to work for the United States government.

She worked as a confidential clerk in the Patent Office of that department until James Buchanan was elected President of the United States. Buchanan was pro-slavery. Anyone with anti-slavery sentiments was an undesirable person in Washington, during his administration. Clara Barton was among the undesirables. With all the other anti-slavery people, she lost her job, but not for too long.

Workers like Clara were hard to find and, after a short while, anti-slave or not, Clara was back on her job. She was there when Abraham Lincoln was elected. She was there when the southern rebels fired on Fort Sumter. She was there when Massachusetts sent its Sixth Regiment to Washington to defend the capital city.

The arrival of the young men from Massachusetts and the war proved to be the turning point in the life of Clara Barton.

She was at the railroad to greet the soldiers. She was with them when they returned from the battlefield, binding their wounds. She enlisted the aid of the citizens of Washington in a drive for money and food for the soldiers of the Republic, and the food and the money came.

Soon, her war work took up all of her time and energy. She gave up her position in the Patent Office. She was at the wharves, the railroads, wherever the wounded soldiers arrived. She washed them, bandaged their wounds, comforted them until the ambulances took them to the hospitals.

It was heroic work. It wasn't enough for Clara Barton. She didn't want to wait till they brought the wounded to Washington. She wanted to be on the battlefield, to nurse the wounded on the spot as quickly as possible.

She went to General Rucker, Assistant Quartermaster of the United States Army, with a plan she had worked out in detail.

There was need for a medical aid corps, nurses to help the doctors where there was fighting, nurses to treat the wounded with minimum delay, nurses to save the lives of the young men at war for their country. She would organize such a corps. There were many women eager and determined to serve the Republic, women who were ready for all dangers, ready to give their lives, if necessary, to serve their fighting men.

General Rucker was properly impressed. He signed the necessary orders, and Clara was quick to put those orders into effect.

She was at the Battle of Cedar Mountain, where she attended the wounded for five days and five nights, almost without any sleep. She was at the Second Battle of Bull Run, tending the wounded, when the orders for retreat were received. She refused to leave before all the wounded men had been evacuated. Exhausted, she fell asleep in the rain, but she did not sleep for long. There was work to be done so long as one soldier remained behind.

Her courage did not go unnoticed. She was acclaimed for her bravery when she finally returned to the capital city. But Clara Barton was not particularly concerned with the praise that was heaped on her. There were other battle-fronts in the war. She was needed, and she would serve.

Abraham Lincoln, in May of 1864, created The United States Department of Nurses. Clara Barton was appointed Superintendent of the Department. Abraham Lincoln, as well as the rest of the country, was well aware of the heroism of the young woman. But more important to Clara Barton was the recognition the country was giving to her nurses-in-arms, to the work they were doing, and the work they were yet to do.

The office of the Department of Nurses was in City Point, Virginia. Clara Barton might easily have spent all her time recruiting nurses and dispatching them to the battlefields. But a desk job wasn't enough for the brave young woman, not while men fought and died in the war. And Clara Barton, that once shy and timid little girl, tended the wounded and the dying until the last shot was fired in that bloody conflict.

She served her country well, during those trying years. At the request of Abraham Lincoln, she continued to serve a while longer in a less bloody, but no less painful capacity. Clara Barton was asked to aid the relatives in the search for men who had been missing in action. For four long and heartbreaking years she reunited the wounded with their families and brought the men who had died home for their family burials.

Clara Barton was near to complete exhaustion, but her work with the war had not yet come to its end.

From all parts of the country, she was asked to come to speak about her experiences in the war, but particularly about the brave role women had played in the conflict.

Each place in which she spoke was crowded with avid listeners. But in each place, her strength grew less and less. She was a tired young woman. She was emotionally and physically worn out. Still, she continued; until she collapsed, seriously ill.

For six months she was kept to her bed.

"No more running around, no more lectures, no more work of

any kind," was the doctor's prescription.

It wasn't a prescription to Clara Barton's liking, but she could do nothing about it.

When she finally got out of her sick bed, the doctor still insisted on his original orders. He didn't want to risk the possibility of a relapse. He sent her to Switzerland, where she was to take a "rest cure" for three years.

It was one thing to take orders; it was another to follow those orders. Besides, even if she had wanted to, the world would not allow Clara Barton to rest.

Only a few weeks after she had settled herself comfortably in Geneva, Switzerland, she was visited by a delegation of the "Committee for the Relief of the Wounded in War." It was the committee which would become the International Red Cross.

The purpose of the visit was to pay respect to the brave young woman. The story of her work had spread across the seas. But the Committee, too, wanted to know why the United States had not joined in their movement, why it was that there was no American Red Cross.

Clara Barton had never heard of the international organization, but she was quick to recognize its importance. She made a promise to work for such an organization the moment she returned to her country.

She might have left at once to work on this new program, but there was a war being fought between France and Germany, the War of 1870. There were men fighting and dying again on the battlefield, and wounded who needed care. Despite all doctors' orders, despite the fact that Clara Barton was far from recovered from her illness, she was compelled to offer her services.

Once again Clara Barton was binding the wounds of soldiers. Once again she comforted the distressed. Once again she put herself in positions of extreme danger. This time her collapse came more quickly. And this time it was her eyes that were affected.

For months she lay in complete darkness, her eyes bandaged against the light. For months she did not know whether she would ever be able to see again. She never complained or regretted for a moment the strength, the energy, the life, she had devoted to the wounded. The return of her sight came as a miracle to her, and she was grateful. She could return to the work she had made for herself.

As might have been expected, when Clara Barton returned to the United States in 1873, she made plans immediately to campaign for an American Red Cross. It was a campaign that was to take ten years, and more; not because of its structure, but because, as the doctors had feared, Clara Barton suffered a relapse in her health, and had to spend the next ten years of her life in a New York sanitarium.

Even in the sanitarium, Clara Barton worked. She wrote letters to influential people, outlining the program of the International Red Cross. She wrote articles explaining its work and values. She would have good friends and an informed public once she got out of the sanatarium and began her efforts in earnest.

James Garfield, President of the United States, was impressed with Clara Barton's plan and argument, and his Cabinet was in agreement. They were on the verge of presenting the proposition to Congress, when an assassin's bullet struck down the president.

But this time there was only a short space of months between Clara Barton's dream and its achievement. Chester Arthur, who succeeded the assassinated president, did not hesitate to press for America's entry into the International Red Cross and, in 1881, Clara Barton became the head of the American National Committee of the Red Cross.

Her work, however, did not stop with the creation of the Red Cross. It wasn't enough for her that the organization went out into the battlefield to attend the wounded. She extended the scope of its duties and obligations. The Red Cross must be ready and willing to serve wherever there was any kind of disaster: fire, famine, flood, or epidemic.

The work of the American Red Cross is well known all over the land. We know of its assistance wherever trouble strikes. It is a hand of mercy wherever it goes, and with it goes the memory of a great American heroine.

Clara Barton survived a frail body, frightful physical experiences, long bouts with exhaustion and illness, for more than ninety magnificent years. She died on the 12th of April, 1912.

What greater memorial to her heroism than the American Red Cross and its great works!

Clara Barton

HARRIET TUBMAN
THE MOSES OF HER PEOPLE

She was one of eleven children born to Benjamin Ross and Harriet Green on a Bucktown plantation on the eastern shore of Maryland. The year of her birth is uncertain—it is thought to be either 1820 or 1821. Harriet Green and Benjamin Ross were slaves. No one kept records of the births and deaths of slaves, only of the price they might bring on the auction block.

The child was called Harriet, after her mother. Sometimes they called her Araminta. When she was five years old, she was put to work. It wasn't the most difficult kind of labor; she pulled weeds, looked after small animals, small children, too; but it was work, and not school.

There would never be any school for Harriet, except the world she lived in. There would never be any pencils, books, reading and writing and arithmetic; her only teachers would be the cruel conditions of slavery and the harsh whips of her masters.

"I grew up like a neglected weed," she said. "I was not happy. Every time I saw a white man I was afraid of being carried away. I had two sisters carried away. One of them left two children."

Harriet, it was said, came from the Ashanti people in Africa. The Ashanti were known for their pride and their rebellious spirit. That pride and spirit were to show themselves early in the life of the young slave-girl.

When she was ten she was brought into the big house at the plantation, to be trained to work as a house-slave. A house-slave didn't have to work in the sun from dawn to dark. A house-slave could always manage to get a little more to eat and better clothes. Still, it was slavery. Instinctively, no matter how much she feared the lash of her masters, Harriet rebelled against those people who owned her, body and soul.

She could never make a bed right, for a master; she could never clean a floor well enough, to please a mistress; dishes constantly fell out of her hands and broke. At the age of twelve, she was sent back to the fields, to chop wood, lift huge barrels and pull stone slabs. She might just as well have been another mule, or an ox, working for her master, but she wasn't. The spirit of rebellion grew and seethed in her; some day it would burst out into the world, for freedom.

An overseer, one of those men paid by the slave-owner to keep his slaves working, was set on whipping a young slave-man for some misdeed, real or imagined. Whip in his hand, the overseer ordered Harriet to tie up the young slave. Harriet, who was fifteen at the time, didn't move. The young slave-man made a dash for his liberty. The overseer picked up a two-pound iron weight and hurled it at the fleeing slave. This time, Harriet moved, and the iron weight crashed into her head.

The blow was enough to kill any ordinary person. But Harriet was no ordinary person. For months she lay in bed, and at times they thought surely she was no more than a step away from death, but Harriet had a mission in life, and slowly she regained her health and strength.

There would be times when the effects of that blow would

return. She would become sleepy, go off into a kind of stupor. It was an affliction Harriet would put to good use. People were inclined to believe she wasn't "all there," that she was half-witted because of these seizures. Harriet let them believe it; there was much she could plan and do under that guise for the good of herself and of her people.

She married John Tubman, one of the few black free-men she knew. Anything and anybody related to that word "freedom" quickened the blood of the young descendant of the Ashanti warriors. But being married to a free-man was not enough for Harriet Tubman. She began to think, talk, and plan escape to the North.

John Tubman, her husband, was not interested. Two of her brothers, Robert and Henry, would join her, then turn back. In the summer of 1849, when Harriet Tubman was 28 or 29 years old, alone, she made her break for freedom.

She traveled at night in the dark. There was money to be made catching runaway slaves and returning them to their masters. She walked through woods, and in water where she could, so that the bloodhounds of her masters could not follow the scent of her trail. At night, she hid where the trees were thick and tall, in the natural caves, and in holes in the ground.

"There were two things I had a right to," she said, later. "I had a right to liberty or death. If I could not have one, I would have the other."

She promised herself that no slave catcher would take her alive, that she would never be returned to slavery.

The way was full of peril; the journey was slow. She moved through Maryland, following the course of the rivers, guided by the North Star. She moved through the state of Delaware, always wary, always alert. At last she crossed the line and into the state of Pennsylvania and freedom.

She knew where she was. She knew that she was free. The air of freedom nearly burst her lungs.

"I looked at my hands to see if I was the same person," she said, "now that I was free."

She couldn't quite believe that she wouldn't change, physically,

Harriet Tubman

too, with her new-born freedom.

"There was such glory over everything," she said. "The sun came like gold through the trees and over the fields."

But there was one cloud for Harriet Tubman in that magnificent moment. She was free, but she had left so many brothers and sisters, so many mothers and fathers behind her; and they were not free.

Great deeds are inspired by such moments of understanding. That moment, one of America's really great heroines was born. With her first taste of freedom, Harriet Tubman resolved to return to the South, to free as many slaves as she could in her lifetime.

It was a little more than a year after her own escape from the slave state that she returned to Baltimore, Maryland. It was a daring venture. The Fugitive Slave Law, only recently enacted by the Congress of the United States, demanded that all United States citizens give aid to any Federal officer involved in capturing an escaped slave. Anyone helping a slave escape was liable to heavy fines. But nothing was to deter Harriet Tubman in her resolve to free her people.

In the winter of 1850, she led her sister and two of her sister's children to freedom. In the spring of 1851, operating from Baltimore again, she led one of her brothers and two other slaves across the Mason-Dixon Line.

Between her freedom forays into the South, Harriet Tubman worked as a domestic servant in the houses of the North. It was the only work for which she had any training. She worked days, and nights, saving her money for the funds her raids required.

She bought herself a gun and some ammunition since she was determined never to be taken alive. She couldn't read or write, but she had friends in the North, who could fake "passes" for the slaves she would free. She even supplied herself with paregoric, a drug to quiet babies, when they needed to be quieted on the dangerous freedom journey.

By 1852, Harriet Tubman had made five forays into the South and led perhaps forty slaves to freedom. Word of her deeds spread quickly through the slave country. The slaves were beginning to call her "Moses." Moses had freed the Israelites from their bondage in Egypt. Harriet Tubman was freeing the slaves from their bondage in the South.

She was a master at the task she had chosen for herself. She was unafraid. The dress of an old woman was her only disguise, she would courageously walk through towns in which her old masters lived. She would carry a chicken, lose it and give it chase, if an old master should cross her path. The confusion and laughter of those standing by would give her just enough time to escape notice and death.

She used familiar religious songs, the seemingly harmless spirituals, to inform slaves of where they were to meet, from where their escape was to begin. She sang songs to warn of dangers ahead, to sound the all-clear, to keep her "train" of freedom riders moving. She was proud of her voice, and well she might have been.

The voice and the courage of the woman freed more than three hundred slaves; the exact number is not known. In the ten years of her freedom, she risked her life making at least nineteen raids back into slave territory to accomplish her mission. The South put a price on her head. They wanted her dead or alive and offered $12,000 in gold to anyone who could deliver her body.

In 1860, Abraham Lincoln was elected President of the United States. In 1861, the South seceded from the Union. The opportunity to free all the slaves was at hand and Harriet Tubman plunged into the crusade.

In the first year of the war, Harriet continued her raids in Maryland. This time there was no Fugitive Slave Law to hamper her. She delivered scores of slaves through enemy lines to freedom. In 1862, she joined Colonel Thomas Wentworth Higginson and his regiment of Negro soldiers, as a scout and nurse, at the request of Governor Andrew of Massachusetts. She trained spies and commandos for that regiment. She was with Colonel James Montgomery, during raids into South Carolina and Georgia.

The most famous of these raids was the one which was begun

from Port Royal and went up the Combahee River.

The Boston newspaper, *Commonwealth,* reported on that raid:

"Colonel Montgomery and his gallant band of 300 black soldiers under the guidance of a black woman, dashed into the enemy's country, struck a bold and effective blow, destroying millions of dollars' worth of commissary stores, cotton and lordly dwellings and striking terror into the hearts of rebeldom, brought off near 800 slaves and thousands of dollars' worth of property without losing a man or receiving a scratch. It was a glorious consummation."

The "black woman," of course, was Harriet Tubman.

Harriet did not like to lose men. She never lost a man, woman or child leading slaves along the Underground Railroad. Harriet Tubman was for life, not death, and throughout the war there was no one more conscious of its cruelties.

"We saw the lightning," she said, "and that was the guns. We heard the thunder, and that was the big guns. Then we heard the rain falling, and that was the drops of blood falling. And when we came to get in the crops, it was the dead men that we reaped."

Only one who loved freedom as much as Harriet Tubman, could reveal such great compassion.

Samuel J. May, minister, educator and abolitionist, wrote of Harriet Tubman, "She deserves to be placed first on the list of American heroines."

Harriet Tubman lived on for almost fifty years after the end of the Civil War. She settled in Auburn, New York, where she tried to build a home for needy black people. She managed to earn enough money to lay the foundation for that home, but no more. She never received one cent for the energies she had devoted to her country. All she ever received from the government of the United States was $20 a month, as the widow of Nelson Drake, her second husband and a veteran of the First Volunteers.

She died in poverty, March 10th, 1913, at the age of 92 or 93 years.

Frederick Douglass, the ex-slave and brilliant abolitionist, wrote to her:

"The most you have done has been witnessed by a few trembling, scared and footsore bondsmen and women whom you have led out of the house of bondage and whose heartfelt, God bless you, has been your only reward. The midnight sky and the silent stars have been the witnesses of your devotion to freedom and your heroism."

Harriet Tubman was buried with military honors. The old body was at rest. But, as with her old friend John Brown, her soul goes marching on.

SOJOURNER TRUTH
A SACRED MISSION

One of the strangest yet greatest voices in the struggle against slavery and for the rights of women in the United States belonged to the eleventh of the twelve children born to Baumfree and Mau Mau Bett.

She was given the name Isabella, at birth, in the year 1797, in the small town of Hurley in the New York Catskill Mountains. Her parents were slaves of Colonel Hardenbergh, a Dutchman. She was sold to a farmer who would whip the youngster regularly. She was sold again, this time to the owner of a tavern and resold to the owner of a plantation.

Under the New York laws of those years, she would in time become free. But Isabella had had enough of slavery. She ran away and found refuge with a family of Quakers. She adopted the name of the family, Van Wagener, and for a while she worked as a domestic.

It was while she was washing dishes, making beds, sweeping floors, that Isabella had a strange experience, a religious experience.

"You read books," she said to preachers and students of the Bible. "God himself talks to me."

She took the name Sojourner Truth. She claimed that it was God who had given her the name and the mission it implied: to travel from place to place, carrying the truth.

For a while she preached in New York City. Then she lived and preached in Northampton, Massachusetts. After which, she traveled all over the country preaching against slavery and for the rights of women.

Sojourner Truth had had no education. She could neither read nor write. But she was a masterful speaker and a magnificent orator.

"Children, I talk to God," she said, "and God talks to me. "'Now, Sojourner,' he says to me, 'I hear talking about the Constitution and the rights of man. I take hold of this Constitution. It looks mighty big, and I feel for my rights, but there ain't any there. Sojourner, there is a little weevil in it.'"

She could reach an audience, make it laugh, make it weep. She could handle her hecklers, and there were many of them, with a tremendous sense for the dramatic.

At one meeting, a white man charged that Sojourner was not a woman, that she was a man in woman's clothing. He challenged that she be examined by some other woman in the audience, backstage.

The meeting went wild. People all over the place jumped to their feet and started yelling at each other. The calmest person in the hall was Sojourner Truth.

"My breasts," she shouted above all the noise, "have suckled many a white babe, even when they should have been suckling my own. Some of these white babes are now grown men, and even though they have suckled at my Negro breasts, they are in my opinion far more manly than any of you appear to be."

Then, dramatically, she ripped the front of her dress open.

"I will show my breasts to the entire congregation. It is not my shame but yours that I should do this. Here, then! See for yourselves!"

In another age, Sojourner Truth might well have become a great actress. Certainly, she had a sense of theatre and she used this in the cause of freedom, freedom for the slave and equality for women.

At an Akron, Ohio women's rights convention she listened to a number of male speakers, each arguing against women's rights, each claiming that women were inferior to men. When she had heard enough, she strode up to the speaker's desk and quickly took over the convention with her deep and beautiful, and sometimes thunderous voice.

"Well, Children," she began, "where there is so much racket there must be something out of kilter.

"That man over there says that women need to be helped into carriages and lifted over ditches, and to have the best places everywhere. Nobody ever helps me into carriages, or over mud-puddles, or gives me any best place! And am I not a woman?

"Look at me! Look at my arm! I have ploughed and planted and gathered into barns, and no man could head me! And am I not a woman? I could work as much and eat as much as a man, when I could get it, and bear the lash as well! And am I not a woman? I have borne thirteen children, and seen most of them sold off to slavery, and when I cried out with my mother's grief, none but Jesus heard me. And am I not a woman?"

Such oratory! Such passion! She could whip an audience into action, and she did, wherever she went, preaching the gospel of freedom.

She was perhaps 65 years old when she served as a nurse during the Civil War. She urged the ex-slaves to leave the South, to come North, where the opportunities for equality were greater. As long as she lived, she battled for her black people. She might well be called the first soldier in the struggle for civil rights.

On the 26th of November, 1883, in her last home, Battle Creek, Michigan, Sojourner Truth died.

"I'm not going to die," she said. "I'm going home, like a

shooting star."

She was ninety years old. Some say she was a hundred, and perhaps older. Whatever her years, she had lived a rich and heroic life, and had left her country a great inheritance.

Sojourner Truth

MARY McLEOD BETHUNE
ADVISER TO THE PRESIDENT

Mary Jane McLeod was one of the seventeen children born to the McLeods in Mayesville, South Carolina. Both her mother and father had been slaves. Mary Jane was born free in 1875, twelve years after the Emancipation Proclamation, ten years after the end of the Civil War; but the every-day life of the black people in the South had changed very little with their new-found freedom.

There was much hard work and drudgery, and no money to speak of. Mary Jane, like the slave children before her, was picking cotton at the age of five. When she walked the five miles to school, at the age of eight, she walked bare foot. The school was an abandoned old shack, with a couple of desks, some old boxes to sit on, a pot-bellied stove in the middle of the room, and a piece of cardboard for its blackboard. However, it was a school, and instinctively Mary Jane knew that learning was the one road to real freedom.

She was a bright youngster and later won a scholarship to the Scotia Seminary in Concord, North Carolina, where she studied for five years. She went on to the Moody Bible Institute, where she was the only black student. She was graduated and headed for New York and the Presbyterian Board of Missions. Mary Jane McLeod wanted to become a missionary for the church in Africa.

"You're too young for the work," they said.

"I'll be back," replied the young woman, but her mission was to lie elsewhere.

For a little while she taught in her own little town of Mayesville, and she discovered that teaching could be both pleasing and rewarding. When the Presbyterian Board of Missions suggested that she teach at the Haines Normal Institute in Augusta, Georgia, Mary Jane was quick to accept the position. The principal of the Institute was an ex-slave, Lucy Laney. Lucy Laney had built that school and, with the aid of the Missions, it had grown. The school and Lucy Laney were to prove an inspiration to Mary Jane.

There were other schools in the South, growing with the aid of the church missions. Mary Jane taught at the Kendall Institute in Sumpter, South Carolina, where she met and married another teacher, Albertus Bethune. She taught at Savannah, Georgia, and in Palatka, Florida. It was in Florida that she decided to follow the footsteps of Lucy Laney. She was going to start her own school for black children. In the fall of 1904, the doors of Mary McLeod Bethune's Daytona Educational and Industrial School for Negro Girls were opened.

The students came and there was a great deal of enthusiasm for the school. But there was no money. Mary McLeod Bethune's dream was on the verge of collapsing before it had really begun. The girls who could afford it paid 50 cents a week for their tuition; it wasn't nearly enough to keep the school alive. Its founder had to find other ways of raising the necessary capital, and she did.

She organized a choral group to sing religious songs and spirituals in front of the white people's hotels; the white people would express their appreciation for the concerts with cash. She approached the richer people more directly, convinced them of her course, and collected a number of sizeable checks for her efforts. She invited still wealthier people to become trustees of her school, and the earnestness of her plea was well received. The Daytona Educational and Industrial School not only survived; it grew.

Eventually it joined with the Cookman Institute for Men, became the Bethune-Cookman College, one of the most respected colleges for men and women in the country. Mary McLeod Bethune was its president until 1942, until the call of her country could no longer permit her to stay in Daytona.

While she was president of the college, she organized the National Council of Negro Women, with headquarters in Washington, D.C. President Franklin Delano Roosevelt recognized the understanding and brilliance of the woman and appointed her to his Advisory Council. He also appointed her Director of the Negro Youth of the National Youth Administration; later, Director of Minority Affairs. During the Second World War he named Mary McLeod Bethune adviser to Oveta Culp Hobby, head of the Women's Army Corps.

Her energy and her work were boundless. She fought against streetcar segregation in the South. She fought against segregation in the hospitals. She fought for equal rights and opportunity for Negroes everywhere. Both Franklin D. Roosevelt and his wife, Eleanor, constantly consulted with her on minority problems and valued both her advice and friendship.

In 1945, after the death of Franklin D. Roosevelt, it was President Harry S. Truman who sent Mary McLeod Bethune to the first organizing meetings of the United Nations in San Francisco. Her title, as she sat and met with dignitaries from all over the free world, was Consultant on Interracial Understanding.

The little girl born to ex-slaves in Mayesville had gone a long heroic way. In 1953, the Spingarn Medal was awarded to her for her great work for the Negro people in the United States. In 1960, five years after her death in 1955, Congress passed a bill, requesting the erecting of a stone monument in her honor. The monument was unveiled in Washington, D.C., January 1st, 1963, exactly one hundred years after Abraham Lincoln's Emancipation Proclamation had declared the end of slavery in the South.

It was a fitting monument, and a fitting time, to commemorate the works of a great lady.

Mary McLeod Bethune

HELEN KELLER
VICTORY AGAINST DARKNESS

She came from an illustrious family. Her father's people had been among the first to settle in Maryland and Virginia. Her mother was related to Edward Everret Hale, the author of "A Man Without A Country." She was born to the comfort of an ivy-covered cottage in Tuscumbia, Alabama, on June 27th, 1880. Ordinarily, she would have led the comfortable life of a young southern belle. She didn't. Fate, illness and handicap intervened and what might have been an ordinary, simple life became one of America's most dramatic and heroic stories.

Helen Keller was a normal child, lovable and bright. She walked before she was a year old, and could even talk, as a baby talks at that age. There was nothing in that infancy to indicate the possibility of the tragedy which was suddenly to strike.

When she was only nineteen months, she became ill, and her

recovery was slow. The illness was a congestion of the stomach and, worse, the brain. For a while it was feared that she would not recover at all. She did, but not without the profoundest loss.

When the infant Helen recovered, it was discovered that she was permanently blind. What was more, she was permanently deaf, as well. Helen Keller was to live in a world of total darkness, and devoid of all sound.

The child, of course, was confused. She could no longer see the faces she wanted to see, the face of her father and mother. Nor could she hear them. When they held her in their arms she could feel their touch and know that she had not been completely deserted.

For her parents, the agony of the misfortune was almost unbearable.

Her mother, Kate, devoted herself to the infant. She walked her in the garden, where she could smell the flowers. She brought Belle, their old setter dog, to the child so that she could touch it and know it was there. These senses were still left to Helen, and her mother helped her understand what she could of the world around her through these senses.

There was Martha Washington, the cook's little daughter with whom Helen played. There was the doll, which later she called Nancy. It wasn't enough. The child grew impatient with the limitations put on her movement and on her ability to understand what was happening all about her. She threw tantrums. There were periods of fitful bursts of temper. These were the only ways the child could express her impatience, anger and frustration.

Kate Keller heard of a Dr. Samuel Gridley Howe of Boston, and how he had educated a woman who was both blind and deaf. She wrote to him immediately, but the reply was disheartening. Dr. Howe had been dead for ten years.

A doctor in Baltimore suggested that she try Dr. Alexander Graham Bell, the man who was developing the telephone. Dr. Bell referred the Kellers to the Perkins Institute for the Blind in Boston. They could send them a teacher who could help their daughter, if anyone could.

The Kellers wasted no time. They wrote to the Institute and, very shortly after, Anne Mansfield Sullivan arrived at the cottage in Tuscumbia. She was to prove the most remarkable visitor, guest, teacher and friend Helen Keller would ever have.

Anne Sullivan had been admitted to the Perkins Institute when she was only fourteen years old, and almost totally blind. She had gone through a series of operations and been partially cured, but not before she had learned the manual alphabet of the blind. When, at the age of twenty, she was graduated from Perkins Institute, she determined to devote her life to aiding the sightless. She was eager to accept the challenge which the blind and deaf Helen Keller offered her.

She brought a doll with her to the Keller household. The doll had been made by blind children at Perkins. Her first lesson for Helen included that doll.

Anne put it into the hands of the six year old child. She traced the word doll on the palm of the child's hand. It didn't work in the beginning. Very little worked in the beginning. Helen was fitful, fought physically with her teacher, refused any of her attentions and rejected her.

Miss Sullivan, however, was a patient woman. She knew the anger which boiled deep down in the child. She took the refusals, the rejections and the physical abuse. She more or less expected them. She knew, too, however, that patience and kindness would surely overcome the resistance and even the antagonism of the handicapped child. And she was right.

She gave Helen the doll again, spelled out the word "doll" on the child's hand. She put the child's hand into water, spelled out the word "water" on the palm of the little girl's hand.

It came to Helen slowly, but once it came to her that there was a relationship between the substance she held and the fingering of her teacher on her palm, the little blind girl began to learn at a phenomenally rapid rate.

She ran to explain to her mother who was overjoyed. She had made a great discovery. She wanted more discoveries. She wanted them fast. She would throw tantrums again, but this time because she wasn't learning quickly enough, because she was impatient with her teacher.

Helen Keller

But Anne Sullivan was pleased. She ignored the tantrums as much as she could. Her little student was able to spell three hundred words at the end of her first three months. She could make sentences with those words. At the end of her six months with the Kellers, Anne Sullivan knew that Helen could spell out more than six hundred words, and was almost ready for reading and writing.

She sent for books printed in braille and was delighted with the way Helen took to them. There was less time now for tantrums; there was not enough time for reading. If she couldn't have Anne for her audience, Helen sought out her mother, or even her old dog, Belle, to spell out on her fingers what she found written in her books of braille.

Anne Sullivan suggested to the Kellers that it was time for their eight year old daughter to meet, play and learn with other children. The Kellers were a bit hesitant, but their faith in Anne Sullivan was unbounded. Helen Keller went with her teacher to the Perkins Institute and her courage and determination soared for the experience.

She communicated with the other blind child by the touching of hands. She would touch many hands, as she grew older, and with a growing love for people from all parts of the globe.

She climbed the monument at Bunker Hill. She touched Plymouth Rock, which marks the landing of the first Pilgrims in America. She walked the sands of Cape Cod in the summer, and let the waters of the Atlantic run through her hands. She was learning all the time.

Helen learned that the deaf could be taught to speak. She insisted that she be taught. Anne Sullivan took her to Sarah Fuller and the Horace Mann School for the Deaf. Sarah Fuller, moved by the eagerness of the ten year old child, accepted the challenge.

It was a most difficult challenge. The learning had to be done almost completely by touch. Helen's hand and fingers were brought to her teacher's tongue and lips for the position of each sound, and to the throat to feel the vibrations.

An ordinary person might have given up quickly. Not Helen. She insisted, in spite of her handicaps and the tediousness of the lessons, that she must learn to use her voice, and she did. Miss Fuller and Miss Sullivan were there to encourage the child.

She spoke when she returned to her home in Tuscumbia; not all could understand her; but she spoke. She would continue to speak, and her voice would be loud and clear in the service of human rights for all people.

Helen Keller was scarcely more than twelve years old when she made her first appeal for funds to aid other blind children. She was no more than thirteen when she raised more than $2,000 for a kindergarten for blind children. At about the same time, she began to write, and the magazine, *Youth's Companion*, printed her inspirational story of her battle against her handicaps.

She enrolled in the Wright-Humason School for the Deaf in New York. She would never relinquish her desire for learning. She studied French, Latin, German, mathematics, geography, as well as lip-reading, and she was a brilliant student.

When she was sixteen, she studied at the Cambridge School for Young Ladies and entered Radcliffe College at the age of twenty.

"I have found that though the ways in which I can make myself useful are few, yet the work open to me is endless. The gladdest laborer in the vineyard may be a cripple."

These were the words and sentiments of Helen Keller, and she gave them to the world.

While she was still a student at Radcliffe, she wrote two books, *The Story of My Life* and *Optimism*. This was one way in which she could work, one way in which she could be among the gladdest in the vineyard.

"I love the good that others do," she wrote, "for their activity is an assurance that whether I can help or not, the true and the good will stand sure."

Graduation from Radcliffe did not bring an end to her studies. She continued to read everything she could. And her work for others had just begun.

She served with the Massachusetts Commission for the Blind and as an adviser on countless other committees dedicated to working for the blind and the deaf. She carried on an endless correspondence with people all over the world, great and small, in her efforts to ease the burdens and problems of her fellow-man.

Helen Keller labored not only for the sightless and those who could not hear, she also gave her name, the respect she had won, and all her energies for the poor, the underprivileged and for peace. Above all, she worked to bring an understanding of beauty to the world.

This brave woman wrote *The World I Live In,* a book in which she spoke of "the small rustle in the tufts of grass," a rustle she could not hear, grass she could not see. But she knew their presence with a knowledge of love, and it was her wish that the world share it with her.

Until the end of her life, in 1968, Helen Keller continued her work. Both her life and her work were an eternal inspiration. In a sense, every organization for the blind, for the deaf and for the handicapped, is a memorial to her work. The men and women who have been moved to carry on against all sorts of odds by the inspiration of the life of this woman are countless.

Truly, the life of Helen Keller is the amazing story of a distinguished American heroine.

MARGARET SANGER
FOR LIGHT AND FREEDOM

Michael Hennessy Higgins carved beautiful saints and angels for the Catholic cemetery in Corning, New York, but he was a freethinker who didn't attend church. He was a rebel. His daughter, Margaret, born in 1883, was cut in his image. But, while her father's rebellion was generally limited to verbal attacks on the establishment, Margaret's life was almost entirely devoted to action.

She walked out of her eighth grade class in Corning because of the taunts of her teacher, never to return to that school. At Claverack College, she antagonized both her teachers and class-mates, speaking out for women's rights and suffrage. She might have become an actress, but she tore up the application the Charles Frohman dramatic school had sent her. The application asked for her physical measurements, and the request offended her sense of dignity.

For a while, Margaret taught school in Paterson, New Jersey, waiting till she was old enough to enter Cornell's medical school. Still intent on a medical career, she became a nurse. It was nursing which changed her life and gave her the course she would follow for the rest of her years.

Nursing took her into the slums of New York, where larger and larger families crowded into the most unsanitary hovels. The men worked 14 and 16 hours a day in a futile effort to feed their hungry children. The women mutilated themselves and died in their attempts to keep the number of hungry children from growing. Margaret was horrified by what she saw. She resolved she would do something about the dreadful situation of these poor people, especially its women.

Margaret met and married a young architect. It was under the name of Margaret Sanger that she wrote a series of articles on "What Every Girl Should Know" for the New York radical newspaper, *Call*. They were intended to provide the kind of sex education which had never been published before in our country. Anthony Comstock, Secretary of the New York Society for the Suppression of Vice, and the Post Office threatened to revoke the mailing rights of the newspaper. The series had to come to an end. The work of Margaret Sanger, however, was just beginning.

She would fight, not only to spread the teaching of sex education; she would challenge the laws which prohibited the teaching of what Margaret Sanger would come to call "birth control."

In March, 1914, she edited and published the first issue of what was to be the monthly *Woman Rebel.* The publication attacked Anthony Comstock, asked women not to have children they were not "physically, mentally or financially prepared to accept or care for," and promised to print information on "birth control."

The *Woman Rebel,* of course, was immediately banned from the mails. Anthony Comstock was a powerful man. Still, with the help of friends, Margaret Sanger was able to get her word around the country. Nor was *Woman Rebel* enough for her. She prepared and had printed bundles of copies of *Family Limitation,* a pamphlet which gave explicit information on birth control.

Family Limitation had still to be released when Margaret Sanger was indicted by the United States Government on nine charges, each of which carried a possible prison term of five years; forty-five years in all. The charges were all really one: obscenity.

Margaret was urged to plead guilty, compromise, and receive a fine or a small sentence. But she would not plead guilty to obscenity. The law, not her work, was the obscenity. Nor would she compromise.

On the eve of her trial, knowing that the law was against her, knowing that she could not continue her work in prison, Margaret Sanger boarded a Canadian boat for England. It was while she was mid-Atlantic that she sent wires to her friends, to release the hundreds of thousands of copies of her booklet on birth control, *Family Limitation*.

In England, she continued her studies in her chosen work earnestly. She discovered that the first book on the subject was written in America by Robert Dale Owen, in 1830. Another American, Charles Knowlton, had written a book in 1832, which provided birth control methods, and he had been fined and jailed for his effort.

More important, Margaret Sanger went to Holland, where Dr. Aletta Jacobs, Holland's first woman doctor, and Dr. Johannes Rutgers had inaugurated free clinics for the poor to teach methods of birth control.

She studied the clinics. She studied the methods. Margaret Sanger was ready to go home to face her trial.

That trial never took place.

While Margaret was in Europe, Mary Ware Dennett, Clara Stillman and Anita Block had organized The National Birth Control League. Public sentiment had built up for Margaret Sanger. That support was to grow to unprecedented heights when the young rebel decided to conduct her own defense in court.

The prosecuting attorney asked for postponement after postponement. The publicity in the newspapers and magazines did not hurt the attractive Margaret Sanger, and did much to spread her message and her cause. Finally, the United States District Attorney, H. Snowden Marshall, issued an order dismissing all charges.

Margaret Sanger

Margaret Sanger was free to work for her cause, birth control.

She spoke all over the country, and everywhere her audiences were large and enthusiastic.

Speaking, however, was not enough. She wanted to bring the knowledge of birth control methods to mothers directly. She opened her first clinic in Brooklyn, New York, in a poor neighborhood. The response was phenomenal. Women came in droves for what Margaret Sanger promised to give them.

One of the women who came for birth control information, however, was a police-woman. Only ten days after her clinic was opened, Margaret Sanger was arrested, and the clinic closed.

"I cannot promise to obey a law I do not respect," she declared, defiantly, in court.

She was sentenced by the judge to thirty days in jail, and the women who crowded the courthouse cried out at the judge, "Shame!"

During her month in the penitentiary, Margaret Sanger talked birth control to the willing ears of her prison mates. On her release, she plunged again into her work.

She founded a new magazine, *Birth Control Review.* She resumed her lectures around the country. She went abroad to England, France, Germany, and as far as Japan. Wherever she went, the women flocked to her appealing for aid.

"The doctor says that if I have another baby, it will kill me."

"I can't feed the mouths of the children I have. How can I have another?"

There was a partial victory when the decision of Judge Frederick E. Crane allowed doctors to give birth control advice to prevent or cure disease. Disease could be interpreted to mean any kind of physical or even mental disorder. For the first time Margaret Sanger could enlist the aid of a physician without his risking the loss of his license to practice medicine.

Dr. Mary Halton, at Margaret Sanger's request, asked permission to teach birth control methods in twenty-nine New York hospitals. Not one hospital would grant that permission. Dr. Rachelle Yarros and Mrs. Benjamin Carpenter needed a court order before they could set up a birth control clinic in Chicago.

Dr. Hannah Stone was refused membership in the New York County Medical Society for her insistence on teaching methods of birth control.

Slowly the work of Margaret Sanger took hold. There were 55 birth control clinics in 12 of the states by 1930. Before 1950, there would be 374 such clinics in the United States and Canada.

The opening of each clinic, however, never came without a struggle. Lecture halls were darkened by the police. There were scuffles with police, too. There were charges and counter-charges. But the lists of Margaret Sanger's friends grew. Clergymen, doctors, newspaper editors, ordinary citizens, let the world know that they respected and supported her work.

In 1931, the New York Academy of Medicine passed a resolution demanding legislation to permit doctors to offer their patients information concerning birth control. In 1936, the courts made it legal to send birth control information through the United States mail. The very next year, the American Medical Association passed a resolution recognizing and supporting the value of birth control education; it created a committee to help the teaching of birth control throughout the country.

The great goal Margaret Sanger had set for herself was at last hers. The need for the teaching of birth control to alleviate the suffering of poor and ailing women was no longer a cause for a crusade. The threat against doctors who offered birth control methods to their patients was completely removed. Clinics to advise women, rich or poor, on methods of birth control, could open anywhere in the United States without fear of raid or persecution. The International Planned Parenthood Federation, which grew out of the dream, the work and the inspiration of Margaret Sanger, does its invaluable work on every continent in the world.

Margaret Sanger labored for the rights of women to have their children when they wanted them until her death, in 1966. Her war for the freedom that comes with knowledge, had moved a long way in her lifetime. It will move still further because Margaret Sanger had a mission and devoted an heroic life to it.

12

ELEANOR ROOSEVELT
A WOMAN FOR ALL SEASONS

The niece of one of America's greatest presidents, the wife of America's greatest president in modern times, Eleanor made nothing of her heritage and her station in life, except for the good of the people, especially the underprivileged people in every part of the globe.

Her father was a younger brother of Theodore Roosevelt. Her mother descended from Philip Livingston, one of the men who signed the Declaration of Independence. Both her parents were handsome young people, prominent in what is called "society." It was to be expected that Eleanor, born in New York City, the 11th of October, 1884, would become part of that "society," full of social grace and with very little contact with the world outside. Eleanor Roosevelt, however, did little that was "expected." She was to become very much a part of the world, and her voice and deeds were to leave an impact on history.

Eleanor was not what one would call an attractive child. She was as plain as her mother was beautiful and her father handsome. She was a shy and withdrawn youngster, but even as a child she was shocked by the poverty around her.

There weren't many opportunities for Eleanor to see how the poor were deprived. It was when she helped her father donate dinners at the newsboys' clubhouse, when she went with her uncle to distribute gifts to the poor at Christmas, when she rode in a coach through the poorer areas of the city, that she got her first glimpses of people who were less fortunate than she was, and her first urge to do something for these people.

Her mother died when Eleanor was only eight years old. Her father died shortly after. She went to live with her grandmother, a grand old lady and very old-fashioned. Eleanor had to wear flannel underwear from the beginning of fall until the beginning of spring. She had to wear long black stockings and high-laced shoes. Her dresses were not like anything the young girls wore to their parties. Everything grandmother did or insisted on only helped Eleanor move further away from people, and further into herself.

There *were* hours of fun for the child. There was always a pet, some toy, an outing with some uncle or aunt, but there were no playmates. Eleanor was an isolated child. She wore a brace to cure a curvature of her spine and braces for her teeth. She was awkward with strangers and not graceful in her movement. Her childhood was anything but happy.

She was sent to school in England when she was fifteen, the Allenswood School near London. For three years she had sympathetic and understanding teachers and children her own age for companions. She was encouraged to play in their games, which she did well, to her own surprise. She was encouraged to participate in all normal school activities, and was pleased to discover that her help and work were welcome and appreciated. For the first time in her girlhood, young Eleanor was really happy.

When she was eighteen, her grandmother called her back to New York. She was at the age, in her grandmother's understanding of the ways of life, for her debut into society.

Eleanor had no interest in either a debut, or society. She wanted another year at Allenswood and then some college. She wanted more of an education than a fashionable finishing school for young ladies could offer.

Grandmother, however, was insistent, and grandmother generally got what she wanted.

Eleanor went to the best social-elite parties, dinners and dances, and all the right places, as her grandmother demanded. But Eleanor was never the life-of-the-party, never comfortable in the midst of all the superficial affluence, idleness and emptiness of the society social. whirl. She drew away from it, and back into herself again. She found some release from this useless kind of life in her outside activities. She went to work, teaching dancing and calisthenics at a settlement house. She worked with the Consumer's League. She made forays into the shops and factories of New York City and reported on their poor safety and working conditions.

One young man of her social set was able to pierce her shyness, her withdrawal. One young man saw the beauty in that tall and sometimes awkward young lady. The young man was the very handsome Franklin Delano Roosevelt, a fifth cousin.

He talked with her about books, music and art. He talked with her about politics and history. He discussed her reports on the factories and the need to improve working conditions.

They fell in love and were married on March 17, 1905. It was Uncle Teddy Roosevelt who gave the bride away.

In 1911, Franklin Delano Roosevelt was elected to the New York State Senate and, of course, Eleanor joined her husband in Albany. It was in the state capital that Eleanor was to begin the life she had always intended, a life devoted to the service of the people.

At first, she limited herself to attending the Senate sessions. She discussed with her husband the debates she heard, and quietly indicated her own thoughts on the different laws under consideration. In the beginning, her thoughts did not go further than the ears of her husband. Soon, however, as she learned more about the ways of politics and gained confidence, she began to speak to others.

Her first audiences were women, but her audiences were to grow very quickly as the career of her husband developed.

In 1912 she attended her first national political convention, a convention which nominated Woodrow Wilson for president. When, the following year, Franklin D. Roosevelt was named Assistant Secretary of the Navy, she moved with him to the nation's capital and quickly became part of the Washington scene.

Eleanor Roosevelt gave birth to six children, one of whom died in its infancy. She had five children to take care of when, in 1917, the United States was drawn into the First World War. Eleanor Roosevelt was a devoted mother; still she found time to serve as a hostess in the canteens for service-men and service-women, to work actively for the Red Cross, and to visit the wounded in the hospitals. Eleanor Roosevelt was appalled by the war, but she did what she could to alleviate the pain and sorrow of the afflicted.

It was a specific visit to St. Elizabeth Hospital for the mentally ill which brought about Eleanor Roosevelt's first battle for governmental reform. The conditions in that hospital were shocking. She reported on those conditions with telling detail. Reforms in that hospital and other government hospitals came quickly.

The action and reaction undoubtedly raised Eleanor Roosevelt's confidence in herself and in her ability to get things done. She was invited to join the board of the New York State League of Women Voters, and she became more and more involved with politics.

Suddenly, in the summer of 1921, that political activity came to a halt. Franklin D. Roosevelt was stricken with infantile paralysis (polio). He survived, but he was faced with a life which threatened to keep him in a wheelchair for the rest of his years. Certainly, this looked like the end of his political career.

Eleanor, however, refused to accept this verdict of defeat. Courageously she helped her husband battle the effects of this dread disease. She did more. She invited people prominent in public life to her home, to dine, talk and confer with her husband on state, national and international problems. She fought for, and was appointed to the position of Finance Chairman of the New York Democratic State Committee. She joined the Women's Trade ·Union League. She took on a lecture tour, speaking primarily to women, urging them to become acquainted with the political scene, with economics and history, urging them to make their newly won right to vote important at the polls.

Eleanor Roosevelt had no political ambitions of her own; she wanted an intelligent electorate. She also wanted to keep the name of her husband politically alive. In 1928, Franklin Delano Roosevelt was elected Governor of the State of New York. In 1932, he was elected President of the United States, and Eleanor Roosevelt was First Lady.

The functions of the First Lady had always been limited to social functions at the White House. Eleanor could handle those functions well enough, but the social life had never been enough for her. She was to change the role of the president's wife drastically.

Franklin Delano Roosevelt was elected during the depression. One-third of the nation was undernourished, without proper housing, without the means to attain proper food and shelter. The President had a giant task to perform: to return the country to some semblance of normality.

Eleanor Roosevelt pitched into that task. She could not recommend or sign national legislation to help better the lot of her countrymen; but she could investigate, report on her findings, and urge her husband to act.

She moved through the work camps and factories. She walked through the slums and slum housing. She visited farms and dust bowls. She even went down the shafts into the mines. There were people who accused her of being a snooper, a gadabout, a meddler. It didn't matter what they called her, the First Lady was intent on getting her knowledge of the country's poverty and needs first hand. She had to know what she was talking about, and when she talked it was with facts, figures and conviction.

Her suggestions to her husband were concrete. He listened

with respect and admiration. Much of the legislation he asked of Congress originated with his wife.

She demanded an end to the destruction of surplus crops, so that it might be given free to the needy. She urged the creation of the National Youth Administration and the Civilian Conservation Corps, both organizations to help the young people in their studies and work. She worked actively with the Works Projects Administration, a project which employed artists, writers and teachers. It created a cultural boom in the country. In addition, the government spent billions of dollars on slum clearance, flood control, rural electrification, projects which were so long in coming.

Franklin D. Roosevelt and his New Deal brought the country out of the worst depression in its history. Eleanor Roosevelt worked hand in hand with her husband. She read his speeches, made suggestions for those speeches, urged and helped him to carry out his programs all over the country. She was especially concerned with the problems of America's minorities.

When the great Negro singer, Marian Anderson, found the doors of Constitution Hall closed to her by the Daughters of the American Revolution, Eleanor Roosevelt resigned from that organization in protest. No white woman worked harder and more consistently for the rights of black people in America than did their white heroine, Eleanor Roosevelt.

The pace and range of her activities increased with the years. She was encouraged by her husband to make her views public, even when she disagreed with his. This led to press conferences, the first time in the history of the United States that a president's wife ever made independent public statements. She opposed, for example, the President's policy of neutrality towards Spain during its civil war. She spoke openly for aid to the Loyalists.

She broke other White House traditions.

She drove her own car, boarded trains, buses and planes alone. She refused to be tailed or protected by the Secret Service. She wrote, in addition to books and articles, a daily column for the newspapers. She spoke at the Democratic National Convention in 1940, and called for unity in the party which was threatening to split wide open, and she won that unity.

In 1941, following Japan's attack on Pearl Harbor and our entry into World War II, Eleanor Roosevelt became Assistant Director of the Office of Civilian Defense. She visited our factories, shipyards and munition plants. Unafraid for herself, she toured the military camps and bases of our fighting forces, wherever they were, in the heat of the Pacific jungles or in Europe.

The call of "meddler" continued to follow her, but it fell on deaf ears. Eleanor Roosevelt had a call to duty, and she answered it.

In 1945, the sudden death of Franklin Delano Roosevelt brought a temporary halt to her worldwide activities. For a while she retired with her grief to her home in Hyde Park. But her country would not allow this great lady to rest for long. Very quickly she was on the road again, her life full, rich, and demanding.

President Harry S. Truman sent her as delegate to the United Nations in 1946. She was a delegate to the United Nations Assembly from 1946 to 1952. She also served as Chairman of the United Nations Human Rights Commission from 1946 to 1951, traveling again all over the world in the service of human rights. Even after her resignation from her posts, she continued her efforts for that peace organization, working as the Chairman of the American Association for the United Nations.

There were the articles, books, and newspaper columns, and an endless correspondence she took care of, letters not only from notables of every country, but the common people, the ordinary people she loved so much.

She worked almost to the day she died, November 7, 1962. She was active at the 1960 Democratic National Convention which nominated John F. Kennedy for president. Her voice, until the end, was loud and clear in the reform politics of New York State. Until the very end, she spoke for working people, for minorities and for peace.

Honors had been heaped on her, while she lived. Colleges and universities awarded her honorary degrees for her humanitarian work. Her face appeared on the stamps of foreign countries for her labors in their behalf. When she was buried, beside her husband Franklin Delano Roosevelt, in Hyde Park, the president, John F. Kennedy, and two ex-presidents, Harry S. Truman and Dwight D. Eisenhower, came to pay their respects and do her honor.

Truly, Eleanor Roosevelt was a woman for all seasons.

Eleanor Roosevelt

AMELIA EARHART
SHE TOOK TO THE SKIES

Almost from the day she was born in Atchison, Kansas, in 1898, Amelia Earhart was on the move. Her father was a lawyer for the Rock Island Railroad. His work took him from city to city, and he always had his family with him. Amelia attended schools in Kansas City, Missouri, Des Moines, Iowa, St. Paul, Minnesota, and was graduated from Hyde Park High School in Chicago, Illinois.

Traveling was always going to be a part of her life, eventually a way of life for Amelia Earhart. She was destined, however, to leave the trains, the wheels, the tracks, the solid earth, for the faster and more dangerous territories of the skies.

For a while, after her graduation from high school, Amelia studied at the Ogontz School, a short distance from Philadelphia. The drive for learning was strong in her. She knew well enough the values of schooling. But a Christmas visit to her sister, who was at St. Margaret's College in Toronto, temporarily cut short her studies.

In Toronto, she saw the wounded Canadian soldiers return from their fighting in the French trenches against their German enemy. She saw the crippled soldiers in the streets, and the young, fresh soldiers ready to embark for the bloody conflict. This was the time of World War I. The United States had only recently been drawn into the battle and just beginning to send over the first combat troops. Amelia Earhart didn't return to school. She found work as a nurse's aid in the Spadina Military Hospital in Toronto. If she could not fight, she would give her aid to the wounded.

It was in Toronto that Amelia Earhart developed her great desire to fly. She had seen planes before and had always been fascinated by their speed, the ease with which they seemed to move through the sky. In Toronto she spent hours watching pilots train for service, and the more she watched, the more she had the urge to learn how to lift a plane into the air and go soaring off.

She asked, but there was no time to teach a woman how to fly, not when the pilots were needed in France. Nor was there the time to take on a woman passenger, though she asked again, when every moment in the training of fighting pilots was so precious.

After the war, Amelia Earhart approached a number of aviation schools. Her heart had become set on flying. But aviation wasn't interested in women at the time, and Amelia's ambition had to wait.

She enrolled at Columbia University and took courses which would lead her to medical school. After a while, though she did well in her studies, she left. She might have made a good doctor, but she wanted to fly.

Her parents, at the time, were living in California near an airfield. Frank Hawks, who would establish two speed records in non-stop flights from Los Angeles to New York, and destined to be killed in an airplane crash in 1938, was the first man to take Amelia Earhart into the air.

There was no turning back now. If there had ever been any doubts, there were none now. Amelia Earhart would fly.

She found herself an instructor, Neta Snook, the first woman graduate of the Curtiss School of Aviation. Learning to fly was an expensive venture. Amelia worked for the telephone company to pay for instruction. She worked five days a week and spent Saturday and Sunday with the plane. As always, she was a good student. She knew her instruments and her motors. She sat in the cockpit and, finally, took her first solo flight.

From the beginning she proved herself an excellent pilot. She belonged in the air.

With some financial help from home, she bought her first plane, a second-hand sports model. She spent as much time as she could with it in the sky. In no time at all she broke the old altitude record for women flyers. She was the first woman granted a pilot's license by the Fédération Aeronautique Internationale.

With her record and her international pilot's license, Amelia began to look for a job. But commercial aviation was still in its infancy, and there were more veteran pilots than needed to fill the need of the young industry.

She was offered one job to fly liquor from across the border in Canada. There was much of this smuggling of liquor into the United States during prohibition. Amelia Earhart would have none of it. She returned to school, Columbia and Harvard Universities. She went into social work at the Denison House in Boston, but did not remain grounded for very long.

She worked at the settlement house, but she kept in touch with her old flying associates. She was a member of the Boston chapter of the National Aeronautic Association and tried to organize a women's flying association. Amelia Earhart would not, could not, forget her flying ambitions, and soon she was called to join a most dangerous mission.

Crossing the Atlantic by plane is a common experience today. Hundreds of thousands of people have done it. But in 1928, Charles A. Lindbergh became an international hero, flying solo from New York to Paris. In 1928, Amelia Earhart was to become the first woman to fly across the Atlantic Ocean.

The plane was a Fokker, christened "Friendship." Its pilot was Bill Stultz. Its mechanic was Louis Gordon. Mrs. Frederick Guest, an Englishwoman of considerable wealth, was sponsoring the flight as a gesture of good will between England and the United States. She wanted a woman aboard that plane. That woman was Amelia Earhart.

The "Friendship" was a three-engine plane, equipped with pontoons, should it be necessary to land on water. It took off with its crew of three, from East Boston, June 5th, 1928. Its first stop was Trepassey Bay, Newfoundland. Here they waited for twelve days, until weather conditions permitted the beginning of the dangerous flight across the ocean.

They took off the morning of June 17th. The seas were still heavy, and there was some question about weather conditions mid-Atlantic, but the flyers were eager to get going. They dropped two hundred of their nine hundred gallons of fuel, to enable the plane to make its take-off in the choppy waters. They lifted the "Friendship" into the sky. They were on their way.

Today, planes cross the Atlantic in six hours or less. But in 1928 there were no such speeds. The jet planes had yet to be developed. The crew of the "Friendship" would be in the air for twenty hours or longer.

In the first hours of the flight they ran into heavy rains and heavy headwinds. Eight hours out of Newfoundland, they lost their radio with no way to communicate with land on either side of the Atlantic, or with any ships which might pass below them.

They had been in the air for almost twenty hours when Bill Stultz announced they were running out of gas.

The crew of the "Friendship" anxiously searched the sea below for sign of land, for sign of land debris, for sign of a boat.

"Is that a fishing boat?"

All eyes strained for the spot.

It was a boat, but how far from land was it?

Another boat, and another, and the crew of the trans-Atlantic plane knew they were near land.

First it was a small island, and then another. Then there was the large stretch of land, the coastline.

Bill Stultz cruised along that coastline for a few miles, looking for a place to land. Then he carefully placed the plane down into the waters. The three intrepid flyers had made the crossing of the Atlantic successfully. They were in Burry Point, Wales.

They were flown to Southampton, then London, and everywhere they went there were crowds to greet them. There were dinners and lunches, and a military parade. Bill Stultz and Louis Gordon received their full share of honors. It was Amelia Earhart, however, who was the greatest heroine of the hour. She was, after all, the first woman to cross the Atlantic by plane.

Back home in the United States, the welcomes and the honors continued. Amelia Earhart kept reminding people it was Bill Stultz who had piloted the plane across the ocean, but they scarcely heard her. She was America's heroine.

The tumult died down after a while, but there could be no more question about the career of Amelia Earhart. She was in aviation to stay.

She became the Aviation Editor of the nationally important woman's magazine, *Cosmopolitan*. She became Vice-President of Ludington Airlines and was called on to lecture on her flight and aviation for women throughout the country. She added to her glory by making a solo flight from the Atlantic to the Pacific, the length or breadth of the United States. She tested autogiros and became a parachute jumper.

G. P. Putnam's Sons, the New York publishing house commissioned her to write a book on her trans-Atlantic crossing. Amelia Earhart wrote *20 Hours, 40 Minutes*. George Putnam liked the manuscript. He fell in love with its author and they were married in 1931.

Marriage, however, could not keep Amelia out of the skies. May 20th, 1932, she set out to fly the Atlantic alone. She started from Harbor Grace, Newfoundland, and for the first hours all went well. Trouble, however, soon began to take over.

First, her altimeter went. The altimeter measures the distance of the plane from the ground. She would have to guess at that distance now.

A few hours later, as the skies darkened, she ran into a heavy storm. The plane began to heave and toss. She tried to lift the plane up over the storm, but it wouldn't climb. There was ice collecting on its wings.

Amelia brought the plane down, as low as she could. The altimeter was gone, so she couldn't tell how close she was to the seas; it was almost like flying blind.

There was more. Suddenly fire erupted from a broken weld in the engine. It surely looked like the end to the gallant flyer. A leaking reserve tank of fuel made a crack-up and death almost a certainty.

Whatever other thoughts ran through the mind of Amelia in those critical moments, the need to go on predominated.

Her eyes moved to the flaming engine. She looked at the fuel leaking from the reserve tank. She strained her eyes for land, any land where she might bring down her crippled plane.

Miraculously, that land appeared, hills and green pastures. As quickly as she could, she maneuvered her plane down. She made a perfect landing. She was in Londonderry, Ireland, exactly 14 hours and 56 minutes after she had lifted off out of Harbor Grace, Newfoundland.

Congratulations and invitations flowed in on the heroic pilot once again. She was the first woman to make the solo crossing of the Atlantic. Only one man had done it before her, Charles A. Lindbergh. She was the only person who had ever crossed the ocean by plane twice. She was not only an American heroine. She was a heroine the whole world wanted to claim.

The English gave her the Certificate of Honorary Membership of the British Guild of Air Pilots and Navigators. The French Senate gave her a tumultuous greeting and the Cross of Knight of the Legion of Honor. The king and queen of Belgium welcomed her and awarded her the Cross of the Chevalier of the Order of Leopold. Back home in the United States, at the White House, she received from the hands of the President, Franklin Delano Roosevelt, the Distinguished Flying Cross.

No woman was ever more honored in the history of the United States, but it was the flying which continued to excite Amelia

Earhart, more than any of the honors heaped on her.

She conquered the Pacific, flying solo more than 2400 miles from Honolulu in Hawaii to Oakland, California. She flew to Mexico City, then from Mexico City to the airport in Newark, New Jersey.

For a while, as Adviser in Aeronautics, she taught at Purdue University. She enjoyed her post of teaching. But there was one more long flight she wanted to make. She dreamed of girdling the globe by plane, the long way around the equator.

Her first effort in 1937 failed. In Honolulu, an accident in the take-off of her plane, the "Electra," stripped its landing gears and sheared off its right wheel.

Amelia Earhart was undaunted. She had the plane returned to California for repairs. Then, with her navigator, Fred Noonan, once again she moved out on her mission.

The "Electra" began its journey from Miami, Florida, the first day of June, 1937. It moved to Puerto Rico, Venezuela, Africa, Karachi and to New Guinea.

Everything went smoothly. There was no hint at all, no sign of impending disaster.

The plane left Lae in New Guinea in good shape. Somewhere near Howland Island, however, an American Coast Guard cutter, the "Itasca," began to pick up distress signals from the "Electra."

The "Itasca" tried to reach the plane, give it directions. For a while there was intermittent contact. Then the voice of the "Electra," the voice of Amelia Earhart, was gone.

The disappearance was complete. Search parties on land, on sea, in the air, could find no trace of either the heroine, or her plane. They could not even find a trace of debris, the kind of debris which is found after any airplane accident. Amelia Earhart, her navigator Fred Noonan, and the "Electra" had simply vanished from the earth.

For weeks, months, even years, it was hoped that Amelia Earhart would still be found alive, perhaps in some remote island or jungle. Theories about her disappearance still linger. No people like to lose a heroine, and so young a heroine. Amelia Earhart was not yet forty years old when the world lost trace of her.

What did happen in that plane, that fateful day? What did happen to its courageous pilot?

These are questions no one will be able to answer with any kind of certainty. What is certain, however, is that Amelia Earhart, in her short life, gave America, and especially the girls and women of America, a heroine who will not be forgotten.

Amelia Earhart

MILDRED DIDRICKSON ZAHARIAS

A STORY OF COURAGE

She was born Mildred Didrickson in Port Arthur, Texas, in 1912, but she was called "Babe," and the name stayed with her throughout her life. It was a name which seemed to fit her more appropriately than Mildred, in all the different areas of her endeavors and her victories. Babe Didrickson Zaharias was the greatest woman athlete in the history of American sports. She was constantly compared with Jim Thorpe, the Carlisle Indian who was perhaps America's greatest Olympic star, and well she deserved that comparison.

Her father was a seaman, a Norwegian who never quite got used to working on land. He had a job in a furniture factory in Port Arthur, but the sea always had first call.

Seaman's pay or factory work, there was never enough money to feed and clothe his seven children, and Babe's mother would take in washing to help pay the accumulating bills.

Nevertheless, it was a happy family, well knit, and love its dominant theme. The Didricksons couldn't give their children very much by way of luxuries, but affection was never missing from their household.

Ole Didrickson, the seaman, was strong on body building. There was a trapeze and horizontal bars in the backyard. He had built them himself, and both the father and his children became expert at gymnastics. Ole also built a weightlifting contraption, to build the muscles of the arms and legs, and the family was good in those exercises, too. As a matter of fact, the Didrickson kids were the best athletes in Port Arthur, and Babe Didrickson was best of them all, boys and girls alike.

She played for the girls' basketball team in Beaumont High School and was high scorer in her very first game. She led her team through an entire season to a record of all wins and no defeats. She had yet to reach her 16th birthday, but she was asked to play basketball for the Employers' Casualty Insurance Company, professionally.

It is common practice for big business firms to organize and support semi-professional sports. Big companies have baseball teams, track teams, even football teams, representing them in sport competitions. The practice serves a dual purpose. It makes for good will among the employees of the company and the town in which it operates; it also makes for good publicity for the business.

Babe was offered a job by the insurance company, so that she could be eligible for their team, and the sixteen year old girl was faced with quite a problem. Taking the job meant moving to Dallas and leaving her family.

There were discussions at home, pro and con, but the job paid $75 a month, and that $75 would go a long way to ease the financial pressures on the Didrickson home. Babe accepted the offer. She sent her mother $45 of that $75, every month. She was also named to the All-American girls' basketball team of the year, and of every year she played for the Employers' Casualty Insurance Company.

The basketball season over, the Babe got permission to organize a girls' track team, and she was a star in every event. She could run, throw the discus, hurl the javelin, high-jump, broad-jump. In the very first meet, she was the winner in eight of the ten events.

She was sent to Chicago, in 1932, to compete in the National Women's Track Championships. She entered eight events, came in first in five of them. When the meet was over, there were three new records, 800 meter hurdles, javelin and high jump; and Babe Didrickson owned every one of them.

In the Olympic Games of that year in Los Angeles, Babe smashed more records. She hurled the javelin 143 feet, 4 inches for a new Olympic mark. She established a new record for the 80 meter hurdles, 11.7 seconds. She placed second in the high jump, the third and last event she was permitted to enter. Along with two gold medals and a silver medal, Babe Didrickson wore the colors of her country with pride at the Olympics, and America hailed a new great star in its world of sports.

Two years later, Babe Didrickson ventured into a new area of athletic competition, golf. In less than five months, she won the Texas Women's Championship. She could drive the ball as far as any man on the golf links. Her ability to get out of the rough, out of a sand trap, her accuracy on the green, was professional right from the beginning. She won championship after championship. She was clearly among the best of America's professional golfers, men or women.

It was on a golf course that she met George Zaharias. She later married him. Unlike so many other women, the Babe took her new name with her, into her profession. She insisted on it. Wherever she went, she was now called Babe Didrickson Zaharias.

Her name was changed, but not her activities.

She pitched an exhibition game for the St. Louis Cardinals. She played ball with the bearded House of David and won game after game for the team with her pitching and hitting.

She played football against Southern Methodist University, in an exhibition game, ran through the line, and passed the ball like a pro.

She was beaten only by Ruth McGinnis in the battle for the National Women's Billiard Championship.

There was no athletic competition in which Babe did not excel. She was a great swimmer and could dive like a champion. They called her "The Queen of Sports."

But, in the midst of all her glory, the great champion was to be struck down.

In 1952, she asked the doctors to explain sudden attacks of weariness. She tired as she walked the green. Her drives were losing distance.

The doctors examined her.

"Cancer."

The diagnosis was cancer. Immediate operation was imperative. The shock was great. The will to live was greater.

The Babe lay on the operating table for four hours while the doctors removed the cancerous tissue which threatened the life of America's greatest woman athlete.

Babe Zaharias made no secret of the disorder which had attacked her. The sportswriters were at the hospital, waiting anxiously for the reports on the surgery.

Had the Babe waited too long for the operation? Would she ever be able to leave the hospital? Would she ever be able to play golf again?

"She'll be able to walk out of the hospital, in time," reported the surgeons. "She'll be able to play golf."

"Championship golf?" asked the newspapermen.

"I doubt it," said the doctor.

The doctor hadn't reckoned enough with the will of Babe Zaharias. It was only a matter of months before the magnificent athlete was out on the course again, and into tournament play.

She won the Serbin Invitation Tournament. She was the winner in the Sarasota Open. She was Number One in the National Capitol Women's Open Tournament. She won the National Women's Open Championship.

The year was 1954. It was one of her greatest years. She had lifted herself out of the gloom of illness, got out of her hospital bed and returned to the playing field. She was the champion.

In 1955, she wrote her biography. She looked forward to many, many years of competitive sport. They were not to be hers. The doctors had removed much cancerous tissue from her body; they had not been able to remove it all.

In 1956, Babe Zaharias, Mildred Didrickson Zaharias was dead. A great American athletic heroine had played well, fought well, left a never to be forgotten mark in the history of sports.

Mildred D. (Babe) Zaharias

15

WOMEN IN WASHINGTON

MARGARET CHASE SMITH
WOMAN IN THE SENATE

The State of Maine has always had a reputation for its fine lobsters. It is also known for its writers. Sara Orne Jewett, Laura E. Richards, Mary Ellen Chase, and Kate Douglas Wiggin who gave us *Rebecca of Sunnybrook Farm* and *Mother Carey's Chickens,* all were born in Maine, or adopted Maine for their home state. But with Margaret Chase Smith, the Pine Tree State gave us the first woman senator in the history of our country, the only woman who has ever served in both houses of the Congress of the United States.

She was born Margaret Chase, December 12, 1897 in the small town of Skowhegan on the Kennebec River. It is scarcely the kind of town one would expect to produce great dreams, romantic gestures and dramatic history. Skowhegan is a rather quiet town, in the central part of the state, and the good people there live their lives in honest work and simple pleasures.

Margaret went to school in Skowhegan. Like so many young women of that time, she taught in the school which she had attended. She also worked as a telephone company executive, and for a newspaper, the *Independent Reporter*. For a time, too, she held an executive position with a woolen company. Margaret Chase didn't become involved in politics until she met and married Clyde H. Smith, an active member of the Republican Party.

Clyde H. Smith was nominated by his party for a seat in the House of Representatives. Margaret Chase Smith worked in his campaign. When her husband was elected, she journeyed to the nation's capital with him, and became his secretary. As secretary to the Congressman, Margaret was involved in the mountains of clerical work produced in committee and sub-committee. As wife of the Congressman, she was quickly aware of all the political forces at work in Washington, D.C., the lobbies, the caucuses, even the social life. It was all experience which would stand her in good stead.

In 1940, Clyde H. Smith died. Margaret Chase Smith returned to Skowhegan, prepared to go back to work for the woolen company, the newspaper, teaching; but Skowhegan had other ideas about this. By a meaningful majority, Skowhegan sent Margaret Chase Smith back to Washington, to take the seat left vacant by the death of her husband. She served in that seat from 1940 to 1949.

She preferred to be called "Congressman," not "Congress-woman." She allowed the proper amount of time for her fellow congressmen to tender their sympathies and their condolences, and their offers of aid, but she knew her way around the capital and plunged into the work her duties and obligations required.

Very quickly, she became a congressman respected for her ideas, for the energy she devoted to her work, for her courageous action. She was independent, and her voice was heard on every important congressional legislation.

She was respected in Congress and by the people she repre-sented. In 1948, the State of Maine elected Margaret Chase Smith to the United States Senate.

This was the first time a woman was elected Senator of the United States. No other American woman has been so honored. And Maine did it in a grand way. It gave Margaret Chase Smith the highest percentage majority in its history. It gave the lady the greatest total vote ever recorded in that state.

In the Senate Margaret Chase Smith extended her good work. She served with the Senate Armed Services Committee, the Appropriations Committee, the Republican Policy Committee, the Reorganization Sub-Committee, and with the powerful Rules Committee. In each, she served with honor and distinction.

She was made a Lieutenant-Colonel in the Air Force Reserve and was awarded the Distinguished Service Award on National Defense. Both honors came for her work in Congress.

There were other awards and honorary degrees for service to her country and its people. It would take pages to list them all. She received degrees from more than 25 colleges and universities.

She received the Voice of Democracy Award, the Freedom Award for Americanism from the Freedoms Foundation and the Political Achievement Award from the Women's National Press Club.

In 1949, 1950, and again in 1954, the Associated Press voted Margaret Chase Smith "Woman of the Year in Politics." In 1967, the United Press International voted her one of the ten most influential women in the world.

In 1964, Margaret Chase Smith declared herself a candidate for the Republican Party's nomination for the presidency of the United States. There was quite a flurry of activity. There were many men and women who would have liked to see her achieve that goal. Women had sought the executive post before, but always with the label of some fringe minority party. Here, for the first time, a woman was seeking the nomination of a major party, one of the two major political parties in the country.

There were speeches and arguments, but this was the year that Barry Goldwater carried the Republican National Party Convention by an overwhelming vote. Margaret Chase Smith didn't get the nomination, but, certainly she opened the way

Margaret Chase Smith

Shirley Chisholm

for some lady, some other heroine of the future, to claim that nomination and get it. It might be said, in all fairness and truth, that Margaret Chase Smith fired the first gun in the battle for the first woman president of the United States.

Margaret Chase Smith has served in the United States Senate for more than twenty-two years. She continues to serve in the Senate, to the honor of all her countrymen, and especially to the honor of the American woman.

SHIRLEY CHISHOLM
A BLACK WOMAN IN CONGRESS

Shirley Chisholm is a woman of conviction, a woman with a mission. She speaks and acts forcibly for all the people, but always she has in her mind, the people she represents, the black community of Bedford-Stuyvesant in Brooklyn, New York and the black people of our country.

Her father was an unskilled laborer. Her mother worked as a domestic. Shirley knew poverty from the moment she was born.

She was born in Brooklyn on November 30, 1924 and when she was three years old, she was sent to live with her grandmother in Barbados. She was eleven when she returned to New York. Economically there was little if any change in her family. Shirley Chisholm was to know need for many years, but she would not allow this to turn her away from the real meaning of her life.

She enrolled in Brooklyn College and received her bachelor's degree. She enrolled in Columbia University and earned her master's degree. She had three great heroines in her childhood. One was Harriet Tubman, the "Moses of her people," the woman who courageously led slaves out of the South to freedom. Another was Mary McLeod Bethune, the black woman who pioneered in education for Negro people. The third was Susan Anthony, the woman who led the battle for woman's suffrage.

In her own way, Shirley Chisholm fights to further the freedom of her people and for equal rights and equal opportunity. She was inspired by Mary McLeod Bethune to pursue her education. She

95

continues the work of Susan Anthony, pressing for women's rights in every area of our society.

Perhaps it was the image of Mary McLeod Bethune that inspired her to teach and sent her to a child-care center in the position of director. Perhaps it was Susan Anthony who turned her to politics, where she could be most effective in attaining her goals.

She was elected to the New York State Assembly, where she served for four years, her community always in mind.

In 1968, she ran for a seat in the House of Representatives, and defeated James Farmer, an eminent spokesman for the black people and former head of C.O.R.E. (Congress of Racial Equality).

Shirley Chisholm speaks without fear and to the point. She truly represents the needs of the people of Bedford-Stuyvesant who elected her to become the first Negro woman in the Congress of the United States.

If anyone thought that going to Washington would change her style, he was wrong. If anyone thought that the Halls of Congress would frighten this little woman from Brooklyn, he was mistaken. Shirley Chisholm let Washington know that she had arrived. She let Washington know that she was going to speak and be heard. She carried the voice of the people of Bedford-Stuyvesant, and it was going to be respected.

She was assigned to the House Agriculture Sub-committee on Forestry and Rural Villages. All congressman are assigned to different committees. But Shirley Chisholm from Bedford-Stuyvesant on an agricultural committee, forestry, rural villages? She thought the idea was preposterous, and it was.

She was interested in urban affairs, in slums, in work for the jobless, in schools for the city children, in help for those who needed it, financially or any other way. She let Congress know how she felt about it. She took the floor in the House of Representatives and called for a change in her committee assignment.

No one had ever before made a speech like hers in Congress. No one had ever questioned the powers that made these assignments. Her speech was without precedent.

Politely, she was asked to withdraw the resolution she had introduced. No less politely, Shirley Chisholm refused to withdraw that resolution.

She wasn't in Washington to hold down a chair; she was there to speak for her people, work for her people.

She received another assignment. She requested the Committee on Labor and Education where she could serve most usefully but was assigned the committee on Veterans' Affairs. It was a committee with which she could work.

More important, Shirley Chisholm had claimed an independence for herself, and for all other freshman congressmen. Her voice was a voice with which to reckon. There could be no doubt in anyone's mind that Shirley Chisholm, first Negro woman in Congress, had come to stay, for a long while, and for the good of her people.

HEROINES WITHOUT SWORD

WRITERS

Not all heroes and heroines slay dragons with spear and sword. There are many who labor in the quiet of laboratory and study in solitude, lonely but unafraid. Our writers, novelists, poets, playwrights, are heroines of this order. Others, unarmed except for their talent and perhaps genius, have brought their voices to the theatre, the concert hall; others to canvas and marble. And there are others who have explored unknown territories of the earth, the sea, the sky, and the mind.

America has such heroines in almost untold number. This volume can present a view of only some of the brighter stars in this galaxy of great women, a look into their lives and the greatness of the work they accomplished.

Anna Zenger, taking the place of her imprisoned husband, in our colonial days, defied the British and defended the precious right of the freedom of speech, publishing her New York *Gazette.*

Phillis Wheatley was brought out of Africa on a slave ship. She was no more than five or six years old when she was put up for auction in a Boston slave market. She was bought by Mrs. John Wheatley, who abhorred slavery and was offended by the sight of a little naked girl being sold. She brought her home and named her "Phillis." Phillis was to be a member of the family.

Mary, Mrs. Wheatley's fifteen year old daughter, took over the teaching of the little black girl, and Phillis was an apt student. She learned how to speak the language of her new land quickly. She learned how to read and write. To the surprise and great delight of the household, Phillis began to write poetry herself, and it was very good poetry.

At first, Phillis Wheatley's poems were a family affair. Phillis wrote about the things she saw, the stories she heard, the troubles the colonies were having with King George of England; a party, a dinner, a letter to young Nathaniel Wheatley who was studying at Harvard. She wrote a poem for Mary, her friend and teacher, to celebrate Mary's wedding; she read the poem to all the guests who had assembled, and the guests were astounded by the brilliance of the work of this young black woman.

She began to give readings of her poetry and was invited into the most elegant homes in Boston for recitals of her work. She gave Mary, who was now Mrs. Lathrop, a sheaf of her poems, enough to make a book. Mary decided they should be published. Phillis Wheatley was only seventeen years old at the time.

Mary Lathrop put her heart into her endeavor to get the poetry of Phillis into book form, but the publishers were skeptical. First they didn't believe that such poetry could be written by a slave-girl. Even when they were convinced, they saw no sales for such a book. Mary was angry, frustrated, but then her concern for Phillis took another turn.

Phillis Wheatley

Phillis, always frail, was not well. She had begun to cough, alarmingly. Mary suggested a rest, a change of atmosphere. Her brother, Nathaniel, was going to England on business and she suggested that he take Phillis with him. The voyage, she thought, would help Phillis regain her health.

Her reception in England was enthusiastic. In December of 1773, A. Bell, Bookseller, published the first edition of Phillis Wheatley's poetry. She was the toast of British society, a black woman who was a poet.

Back in America, trouble was brewing between the colonists and the Mother Country. It burst into flames, almost as soon as Phillis returned to Boston.

There was fighting at Bunker Hill. General George Washington was forced to retreat. The frail Phillis Wheatley went out many nights to nurse the American wounded. When she heard that George Washington was camped on the other side of the river, she sat down to her desk and wrote a poem in his praise:
"Famed for thy valour, for thy virtues more. . . ."
and she crossed the river to deliver the poem to one of the General's aides. She received a long and humble letter from Washington, in which he expressed his gratitude, praised her poetry, invited her to visit with him.

The poem was printed in the April, 1776 issue of the *Pennsylvania Magazine,* together with the letter that General Washington had sent the poet.

She wrote much, but she published little. The country was torn by war. Death came to Mary and Nathaniel, to Phillis' child, born after she had married John Peters. John Peters had fought heroically in the American Revolution, but debts put him into prison. Phillis was ill and alone.

Death came to Phillis, too, December 5th, 1784. Like with so many writers before her and after, the rewards for her work were late, too late, in coming.
"Should you, my lords, while you peruse my song,
Wonder from whence my love of Freedom sprung,"
she wrote in one of her earliest poems.

Clearly, we do not speak or write in such phrases today, but the feeling in those words, the sentiment, the passion, are of America. Black and brought to this country as a slave, certainly Phillis Wheatley must be counted a bright star in the galaxy of American heroines.

Harriet Beecher Stowe was another such star. She was born in June, 1811, in Litchfield, Connecticut. Her father was a minister. Her mother, who died when Harriet was five years old, had taught school. Faith and learning, along with love, were the basic elements in the Beecher household, and Harriet was well imbued with them. She also learned to loathe the institution of slavery.

She attended school in Litchfield, then went to her sister Catherine's Hartford Female Seminary, to continue her studies and to teach. When their father became president of Cincinnati's Lane Theological Seminary, both sisters joined him in Ohio, and opened another school for young ladies. It was here that Harriet met and married Calvin Ellis Stowe, a brilliant young educator.

Ohio, bordering on Kentucky, felt the full brunt of the antagonism between the slave states and the free states. The students at the Seminary were from both the North and the South. Argument was the order of the day and, too often, the debate erupted into violence. Slaves, seeking freedom, moved into Ohio from Kentucky, and then north. Sometimes they remained in Ohio, with the free black people. Occasionally they were helped by southern students, as well as those from the North. More often, they were attacked and their houses burned.

It was during this period that Harriet Beecher Stowe taught black children in her own home, and raised money to buy the freedom of captured runaway slaves, all with the approval of her husband.

In 1850, her husband was offered the post of professor of religion in Bowdoin College, in Brunswick, Maine. It was a long way from the bloodshed of the Ohio-Kentucky border. The Stowes were glad to be away from the immediate violence, but the question of slavery was not to be dismissed.

It was in Bowdoin that Harriet Beecher Stowe wrote the first chapters of *Uncle Tom's Cabin*. She sent the first pages of the

Julia Ward Howe

Harriet Beecher Stowe

manuscript to the *National Era,* a Washington magazine, and they quickly contracted for the entire book. It was published in serial form from June, 1851 to April, 1852, and in book form in 1852. In one year, more than 300,000 copies of the book were sold.

Although there were some abolitionists who objected to some of the gentler scenes in the book, *Uncle Tom's Cabin* proved to be the most powerful anti-slavery force in the country. It stirred the country into a state of wrath. The forces against slavery, armed with *Uncle Tom's Cabin,* pressed more vehemently than ever for the end of slavery; the slave states reacted as violently. Nothing moved the country more to the ultimate question, the war, and the end of the slave blight, than did the work of Harriet Beecher Stowe.

She was the recipient of praise and honors from both sides of the Atlantic. She continued to work for freedom. She wrote novels, hymns and travel books, but nothing she did would approach the strength and power of *Uncle Tom's Cabin.* Harriet Beecher Stowe had made her contribution; it is a contribution that will live forever in the history of our country.

Edith Wharton, born in New York City in 1862, was the first woman to win the Pulitzer Prize for literature with her novel, *The Age of Innocence,* in 1921.

Edna St. Vincent Millay was born in Rockland, Maine in 1892. She was a great lyric poet. The literary world compared her work with the brilliant romantic poets of the time of Shakespeare. She was the first woman to be awarded the Pulitzer Prize for Poetry, in 1923. A graduate of Vassar College, sensitive to the world about her, she "burned the candle at both ends," as she wrote in her poetry. She died in 1950.

Pearl Buck was born to a family of missionaries in Hillsboro, West Virginia, in 1892. She was only sixteen years old when she was graduated from Randolph-Macon Woman's College in 1914. Following the footsteps of her parents, Pearl Buck did missionary work, mostly in China, for the next twenty years.

She began to write novels based on her work. In 1930, her *East Wind: West Wind* was published. Her second novel, *The Good Earth* established Pearl Buck as a literary figure of world stature.

Pearl Buck

The Good Earth brought her the Pulitzer Prize in 1932. The novel was dramatized that year. It was made into a movie with Luise Rainer who won the Oscar in 1937, as the best actress of the year, for her acting in it.

There were more novels, *The Exile, The Fighting Angel, The Patriot, Dragon Seed.* In all her work, she teaches understanding of the customs and the problems of the East. She preaches tolerance, love, and good will.

In 1938, Pearl Buck was awarded the Nobel Prize for Literature, the first and only American woman so honored.

Pearl Buck's missionary work is not ended. She continues to write, continues her good influence for the good of mankind and for peace.

Rachel Carson, in a world that has only recently become acutely aware of ecology, the science of environment, the pollution rampant in the world, and its threat to our very existence, stands as a great and prophetic figure. Her great work in this field provided the start of intensive investigation and the beginning of essential action, to clear the air, clean our waters, and better our environment. She may well prove the saint who sounded the warning and awakened the people to salvaging the beautiful world around them.

She was born in Springdale, Pennsylvania and received her bachelor's degree at the Pennsylvania College for Women, and her master's degree in biology at Johns Hopkins University.

Her love was science. She taught biology at the University of Maryland, and worked for sixteen years with the United States Fish and Wildlife Service. She became editor-in-chief of its publications. It was while working in the government service that Rachel Carson began to write the books which were to make such great impact on her readers.

The Sea Around Us was the first book to arouse interest in her thoughts, her ideas, her perceptions. It brought an immediate and praiseful reception. "Once or twice in a generation does the world get a physical scientist with literary genius," *The New York Times* critic reported. It was the general opinion. This important work was widely read throughout the world.

Rachel Carson

An earlier book, *Under the Sea Wind,* was reprinted and immediately became as popular as *The Sea Around Us.*

The Edge of the Sea, her third book, added to both her esteem and the public demand for her work.

It was Rachel Carson's *Silent Spring,* however, her fourth book, which created the great sensation.

Her first works were on the beauty of the world around us, our environment, and how this beauty affected our lives. *Silent Spring* turned the picture around and, dramatically, demonstrated how man was destroying this beauty around him, his environment and life.

As a biology student, she had studied genetics, the science of heredity. As a biologist with the United States Fish and Wildlife Service she had been concerned with the new and powerful insecticides which the government, farmers and individuals were beginning to use in their battle against harmful insects. What Rachel Carson discovered shocked her. We were destroying the insects, but we were also killing fish, birds, polluting waterways, and most harmful of all, the vegetation, the food we eat. Actually, we were slowly but surely poisoning the environment and poisoning ourselves.

The reaction to Rachel Carson's *Silent Spring* was immediate and sometimes violent. She was attacked, called a sensationalist, a publicity-seeker, a distorter of the truth. She was supported and defended by those who knew better. But neither the attack nor the defense was as important as the principal result of her work, a public awareness of the problem of pollution, and the demand on the part of the public that the problem be met and resolved.

There is widespread pollution now, in our atmosphere, our water, and the air we breathe. This is a fact that has been known for some time. It is also a fact that little, if anything, was done about it.

The story is different today. The pollution remains and perhaps grows, but the situation will not remain as it is. From the White House to the man in the street, pollution has become perhaps the major domestic problem. It will be met and attacked. Perhaps, it will be eradicated. And Rachel Carson will be honored as the woman who pioneered in this great work.

In 1952, Rachel Carson was presented with the Distinguished Service Award of the Department of Interior. In that same year, she received the National Book Award for non-fiction.

There were other awards: the Frances Hutchinson Medal of the Garden Club of America, for her service to conservation; the Gold Medal of the New York Zoological Society; the John Burroughs Medal; and the Gold Medal of the Geographical Society of Philadelphia.

Rachel Carson died in April, 1964, less than two years after *Silent Spring* was published, but not before she had begun to see that the message of her book had reached the people, and that the people were responding.

This is the reward Rachel Carson reaped from her work. What greater rewards lie in store for the name and the contribution of this great American writer and scientist depend so much on the preservation of the beauties of our environment, the beauties she so magnificently portrayed.

HEROINES IN THE THEATRE

There is a special courage required to be able to perform before an audience, especially an audience which has paid to be amused, delighted, or experience a deeply moving moment. It requires even greater courage to battle one's way to stardom in any of the different branches of the theatre. It is even courageous just to think of making the theatre one's profession, with all its built-in uncertainties and the tremendous competition.

Yet, the number of American women who have ventured into the life of a dancer, a concert artist, an actress, would fill the pages of a good-sized telephone book. The number who succeeded is very small by comparison. Still, there were many women who created unforgettable roles in plays, women whose voices will never be forgotten, and women who opened new paths for their art.

Maude Adams was born in Salt Lake City, Utah, in 1872. Her name was Kiskadden, but she assumed her mother's maiden name as an actress. She left school at the age of 16 to join the famed E. H. Sothern troupe of actors. At the age of 20, she played a supporting role for the great John Drew in *Masked Ball*. Her first starring role was in James Barrie's *Little Minister*. Her most famous role was *Peter Pan* in that most loved of all of Barrie's plays.

Maude Adams contributed more than her acting to the theatre. She developed new lighting techniques and, when she retired from active performance, she turned to the teaching of drama at Stephens College in Columbia, Missouri.

Ethel Barrymore was the daughter of Maurice Barrymore, an actor, and Georgiana Drew Barrymore, an actress. Her grandfather was the magnificent John Drew. She was born into a family of actors. Her brothers Lionel and John were both matinee idols. Ethel, born in Philadelphia in 1879, was a great actress herself, a first lady of the theatre.

She made her first professional appearance at the age of 15. She was a star at the age of 22. Her whole life, until death in 1959, was devoted to the theatre. Her dignity, the depth of her performance, the range of her work, made Ethel Barrymore one of the theatre's truly great performers.

Katherine Cornell reached stardom in the classical manner, by way of a dream, ambition, and hard work. She was born February 16, 1898, in Berlin, Germany, where her father was taking post-graduate studies in surgery. But Dr. Cornell, like his father, was more interested in theatre than in anything else. He bought the Majestic Theatre in Buffalo, New York, and quit medicine. Katherine came by her love for the theatre naturally. She was only a child when she saw Maude Adams in *Peter Pan* and decided upon her career instantly.

Her first role as an actress was with the Washington Square

Helen Hayes

Players in New York. She had exactly four lines in the play, *Bushido.*

Getting work in the New York theatre was no easier then than it is today. Katherine went out with a stock company. She was ready to do any kind of acting to learn and become proficient in her profession.

Her first "break" came in the fall of 1921, in *A Bill of Divorcement.* She was recognized at once as a "star of the future." The future was not too long in coming. She played a lead in *The Green Hat* and her name went up in lights on the theatre's marquee.

Success followed success, but Katherine Cornell's greatest role was that of Elizabeth in *The Barretts of Wimpole Street.* Perseverance, devotion, and hard work was the recipe for this great lady's success in the theatre. Her history in the theatre serves as a living model for all, men and women alike, who aspire to a career on the stage.

Minnie Maddern Fiske was born in New Orleans in 1865 into a family of actors. When she was only three years old, she appeared in Shakespeare's *Richard III.* She played the part of an old lady in *Lady of Lyons* at the age of thirteen, and was performing as a star when she was fifteen years old.

Always a grand lady of the theatre, she boldly undertook the leading role in Henrik Ibsen's *A Doll's House, Ghosts,* and *Hedda Gabler.*

Minnie Maddern Fiske was not only a great actress but knew that the theatre could survive and grow only with new ideas, brave conceptions, and willingness to present and cope with contemporary conflicts. Until her death in 1932, Minnie Maddern Fiske gave herself to this kind of theatre which, in time, was to give America such great playwrights as Eugene O'Neill, Tennessee Williams, and Arthur Miller.

Helen Hayes, more than any other actress today, is introduced to her audiences, in or out of the theatre, as its First Lady. She merits the title. She has earned it, not only for her brilliant career as an actress, but for all her untiring efforts in behalf of her profession as well.

Helen Hayes was born in Washington, D.C. in 1900. In 1909, before she was nine years old, she made her professional Broadway debut in the musical comedy, *Old Dutch.* She appeared in a number of Broadway musicals until 1914. In that year, she was the juvenile, playing with the great actor, John Drew, in *The Prodigal Husband.* Her first starring role came in 1918, in *Dear Brutus.*

It was her Cleopatra, however, in *Caesar and Cleopatra,* that brought her into stardom, in 1925. She followed this stellar performance with an equally brilliant performance in *Mary of Scotland.* Her Queen Victoria of England in *Victoria Regina* established her as one of the greatest actresses in the history of American theatre.

Though her whole life has been theatre, the work of Helen Hayes did not begin and end with the rise and fall of the curtain. She devoted much of her endless energies in behalf of the young actors and actresses, through personal effort, and in her work with theatrical organizations. Her efforts have not gone unnoticed. No one is more respected, more loved, in her profession, the theatre, to which she has given and continues to give so much.

Ethel Barrymore

MARIAN ANDERSON
THE MAGNIFICENT VOICE

America has produced many great singers for the concert halls
and opera house, but the one voice, the voice of the century,
belongs to the gracious and most humble Marian Anderson.

Her mother had been a schoolteacher. Her father delivered coal,
ice and wood. Marian, their first child, was born in one of the
poorer sections of Philadelphia, Pennsylvania, in 1907. The only
luxury the family could afford was the luxury of music. More
exactly, it was the music of the church which the family sang
together, not only on Sundays in worship, but at home, as the
spirit moved them. The spirit moved them often, and they made
beautiful music. The family was blessed with good voices, if with
nothing more.

Marian fell in love with a violin she saw in a pawnbroker's
window. The violin cost $3.98, a huge sum for the little girl who

was only six years old. But determination was inherent to the character of Marian, even as a child. She ran messages for the neighbors, swept doorsteps, and scrubbed till she had amassed the huge sum of $3.98 to buy the violin.

The instrument, of course, was not a good one, but Marian learned to play it. She learned to play the second-hand piano which came into the American household, too. It was a foregone conclusion that Marian was headed for a musical career. It was not, however, the violin nor the piano which would carry Marian Anderson to the concert stage, and beyond. It was the rich and beautiful contralto voice with which she had been born.

She sang in church, in local clubs and societies when she was only eight years old. She was that wonderful "Ten Year Old Contralto." She had enrolled in a commercial high school in Philadelphia to learn short-hand and typing to help ease the financial burdens at home, but the principal of the school heard her sing and recommended her to a high school where she might develop her musical abilities.

A voice, no matter how good, needs training for concert work. Fortunately for the world, the Philadelphia Choral Society provided Marian a scholarship to continue her studies in voice. She could not have gone without the scholarship. Her father had died and her mother was scarcely able to bring in enough to feed her family.

Marian studied with two great teachers, Agnes Reifsnyder and Giupseppe Boghetti. She learned quickly and well. In 1923, her teacher entered her in a contest for soloists sponsored by the Philadelphia Philharmonic Society. Marian won that contest at the age of eighteen.

Two years later she was first in a second contest. Her reward was a solo appearance with the famed New York Philharmonic Symphony Orchestra in New York's Lewisohn Stadium.

Her next step should have been a concert tour through the United States, but Marian Anderson was a Negro. The concert managers were quick to recognize the genius of the young woman, but there was the money that was needed for traveling and for hotel rooms. There were towns and cities which had no accommodations for a black woman, even if she profoundly moved their citizens with her extraordinary voice.

Marian decided she might do better in Europe. A Julius Rosenwald Fellowship provided her with funds to study abroad for four years. She studied and gave a concert in Berlin. She sang in Norway, Denmark, Sweden, for their kings and their people. She sang at the home of the great Finnish composer, Jean Sibelius, who marveled at her voice and her interpretation of his work. She sang in France and in England. In Russia they begged her to stay.

Everywhere she went there were wild applause and ovations. Her greatest compliment came from Arturo Toscanini who was considered the greatest conductor of symphony orchestras at the time.

He said, speaking of the voice of Marian Anderson, "It is a voice one is privileged to hear only once in a hundred years."

Marian Anderson returned home in triumph. She would sing again in Europe, in Africa, in South America, but she was glad to be back with her own people.

Her reception in the United States echoed her reception in Europe.

"One of the great singers of our time."

"Mistress of all she surveys."

One ugly incident threatened to mar her return. The organization of The Daughters of the American Revolution, forgetting it was freedom for which their forebears fought, would not permit her to sing in Washington's Constitution Hall.

The reaction of the people was immediate. The Daughters of the American Revolution were attacked for their display of racism by ministers, musicians, and newspapers. Eleanor Roosevelt immediately sent in her resignation from the organization. Harold L. Ickes, the maverick Secretary of the Interior, made a more positive gesture. He invited Marian to sing in the open air, to the multitude he promised would gather around the Lincoln Memorial in Washington, on Easter Sunday.

Marian Anderson sang from the Lincoln Memorial, and her voice was carried all over the nation by radio, for those who

116

Marian Anderson

could not be present. There is a mural in the building of the United States Department of Interior commemorating the great event.

There were more concerts, more tours. In 1957, the State Department sent Marian Anderson on a good-will tour to the Orient. She traveled some forty thousand miles and sang in China, Japan, Korea, the Philippines, Malaya, India. In 1959, President Dwight D. Eisenhower named her United States delegate to the General Assembly of the United Nations.

Honors came from everywhere for Marian Anderson. She was awarded the coveted Spingarn Medal for her achievements. She was awarded the Bok Award from Philadelphia, for the honor she had brought the city in which she was born. Howard University awarded her an honorary degree in music, as did Smith College and Temple University, among others.

Perhaps, however, most gratifying to Marian Anderson was the creation of the Marian Anderson Scholarship to aid young singers in their studies.

A great person, a humble person, "a voice one is privileged to hear only once in a hundred years," this is Marian Anderson, her work, her art, her great and enduring goodness.

GEORGIA O'KEEFE

ARTIST

America has produced its number of notable artists and sculptors, but women have not been particularly in the forefront of the art world, except in the business of running art galleries. There is one woman, however, who has drawn worldwide attention, respect and honor, with her work on the easel. That woman is Georgia O'Keefe.

She was born in Sun Prairie, Wisconsin, in 1887. She studied at the Art Institute of Chicago and at the Art Students League in New York. For a while she worked as a commercial artist, but her vision reached beyond the commercial. She studied at the Teachers College of Columbia University, and taught art in Texas and South Carolina; but it was painting, rather than teaching, which would be her life.

Alfred Stieglitz, the famous photographer, was the first to show the work of Georgia O'Keefe in New York. Her paintings of flowers and landscape drew the immediate attention of art-lovers and art critics. Her concepts and her execution in brilliant colors were daring and wholly original. From the beginning, she was acknowledged an important American painter.

The Museum of Modern Art exhibited her work in its attempt to define the meaning of "modern" in contemporary painting. She was one of nineteen artists in the exhibition.

The Metropolitan Museum of Art, the Brooklyn Museum, the Tate Gallery of London, among other important institutions, bought and exhibited her work. Thomas Craven, noted art critic, called her "the foremost woman-painter of the world."

America hasn't many women artists, but it does have Georgia O'Keefe.

Georgia O'Keefe

MARGARET BOURKE-WHITE
LADY WITH THE CAMERA

She was born in New York City in 1906. She intended to become a biologist but when she was a junior at college, her father died and that ended her studies. She needed a job. She turned to photography, and the career of Margaret Bourke-White was started.

She became an industrial photographer, and the clarity of her pictures and their documentary value were immediately apparent. She had no difficulty getting work. She was particularly good at picture stories popular in such magazines as *Look* and *Life*. She became one of the top photographer-reporters in the country.

Life sent her to Russia. She covered World War II for *Life* in England, Romania, Turkey, Egypt and Syria, in addition to China. She was on the battlefields in Italy and France. Margaret was just about 20 years old when she started to use her camera professionally. She was the most respected woman with a camera by the time she reached her 23rd birthday. At 27, she was ranked one of the best photographers in the world.

She was on an assignment in Japan when stricken with a serious nervous disease causing her to stagger and lose her balance. Her hands and her fingers were unsteady and she was unstable on her feet. It seemed to be the end of her career, and she was still a young woman.

The doctors diagnosed the disorder.

"Parkinson's disease."

The doctors have known the symptoms for a long time but have not discovered a cure for the dread disorder.

They prescribed exercise, walking four miles a day and other therapy for the hands, the wrists, the fingers.

Nothing helped.

There was one possibility left to Margaret Bourke-White, a brain operation, a dangerous brain operation.

The doctor couldn't promise success. The operation sometimes, but only sometimes, effected a cure. Death was always a possibility in brain operations.

Margaret listened as the doctor talked, but her mind was made up. She was not immune to fear, but she had sat at the topmost edge of the tallest buildings to get the photograph she wanted, had flown through enemy flak, and crawled under tanks in the midst of murderous gun-fire. She had never avoided risks in her work. She was not about to run away from a risk when her career and her life were at stake. She asked for the brain surgery.

The story, fortunately, has a happy ending.

Margaret Bourke-White was one of those few lucky people who were helped by the brain surgery. The help, however, does not come all at once. First, it was an arm which moved completely under control. Then her back loosened, and she could straighten it. She could walk again. This all took time; and there was more.

There was therapy to strengthen her arms and legs, therapy to strengthen her fingers. There was therapy, too, for the muscles in her throat. She had to learn to talk again so that people could understand what she was saying.

Margaret Bourke-White was endowed with tremendous courage. It was no time at all, as we measure time in such circumstances, before she returned to her job at *Life*.

The art of her camera has won acclaim for Margaret Bourke-White throughout the world. Her work, and her life, must prove an inspiration for all of us who dare and do.

Margaret Bourke-White

MARIA MITCHELL
WATCHER OF THE SKIES

Nantucket is a little island, 14 miles long, 3½ miles wide, just south of Cape Cod, Massachusetts. During the winter, it is a quiet retreat from the rush and noise of city life. Sometimes, when the channel of water separating Nantucket from the mainland freezes, the little island is completely isolated.

It wasn't always that way. At one time Nantucket was a thriving port for the whaling industry. There were always whalers docked, about to set out on a voyage or just returned. Ships unloaded their cargo. Ships took on provisions. Captains checked their chronometers which are very accurate time-pieces the whaling captains used to check the position of the stars. It was the position of the stars which told them where they were, in what direction they had moved. William Mitchell, watchmaker and astronomical observer for the United States Coast Survey, was a very important citizen in Nantucket in the days of the whalers. It was to William Mitchell, in 1818, that a daughter, Maria, was born; and Maria was destined to become the first great American woman-scientist.

When she was still a very young girl, her father's telescope enchanted her. She inherited her father's love for mathematics and she was a quick learner. As a child, she could adjust a chronometer by the stars, a most difficult task, and do it with great skill and accuracy. At school, she was considered a mathematical genius.

She taught school for a while and worked as a librarian. Her love, however, was the skies and she spent countless hours at her father's telescope.

One night, Maria Mitchell noticed an unfamiliar light in the sky. It was a light that, by all her calculations, should not have been there. She rechecked her books and suddenly the truth dawned on her. She had discovered a new comet in the sky.

Quickly she called her father. It was like discovering a new land. Her father peered into the lens of the telescope. Maria was right. It was a comet, and it was the first time any man or woman had looked at this comet through a telescope.

He noted it in his log book. The time was ten-thirty in the evening of October 1, 1847.

The date and the time were important. Frederic VI, King of Denmark, had offered a gold medal for the discoverer of a telescopic comet. William Mitchell wrote a letter detailing the discovery of Maria Mitchell to Professor William Bond of Harvard. The letter was mailed in the morning. There was only one hitch to the joy in the Mitchell household. Was there someone else, another astronomer, who had discovered that comet first?

There were two astronomers who did find that comet in their telescope. There was Father da Vico of Rome, and a Mr. Dawes in England. But Maria Mitchell was the first to discover it, by only a few days, and those few days were most important. In 1848 Maria Mitchell received the coveted award from Denmark. At the age of 30, Maria was the first woman in America to be honored

Maria Mitchell

as a professional astronomer.

There were more honors. That same year, Maria Mitchell was the first woman to be elected to the American Academy of Arts and Sciences. In 1850, at the age of 32, she became the first woman elected to the American Association for the Advancement of Science.

In 1865, she became Professor of Astronomy at Vassar Female College. She taught at the college for many years, and a number of her students went on to gain their own fame in astronomy.

She was 71 years old when she retired in 1889 and died the same year.

In 1922, Maria Mitchell was elected to the Hall of Fame, the only woman scientist in America's shrine to the accomplishments of its people. Astronomer and teacher, Maria Mitchell had made her contribution to the history of America, her life one more chapter in the story of the greatness of its women.

CORETTA KING
"WE SHALL OVERCOME"

In the 1960s, three great Americans fell, killed by assassins' bullets. One was the President of the United States, John F. Kennedy. The second was Martin Luther King, Jr., winner of the Nobel Prize for Peace. The third was Robert F. Kennedy, brother of the assassinated president and candidate, himself, for the presidency of the United States.

Each of the three men had a dream. Each was a hope for the young people of America. Martin Luther King, Jr. was a hope for all the black people of America.

No one who lived in those days, no one who saw on the screens of their television the moments and the days of mourning, will ever forget the three heroic wives of the fallen leaders: Jacqueline Kennedy, Coretta King, and Ethel Kennedy. Our sorrow was deep. Our sympathies went forward to the three

Coretta King

courageous women. Their faces were paled, their eyes strained with their enormous grief, but their bearing was classic. Violent death had robbed them of their husbands, yet they stood and walked with the nobility of the truly great.

Perhaps Jacqueline Kennedy and Ethel Kennedy had allowed thoughts of such a moment to pass through their minds, only to dismiss it quickly. Coretta King had lived with the threat of sudden death, for herself, her husband and her children for a long time.

She was born Coretta Scott in Heiberger, Alabama, on April 4, 1927. Her father operated a small country store and hauled lumber, to keep his little family housed, clothed, and fed. Her mother helped, too. She drove the local school bus. Coretta never went hungry, but there wasn't enough money at home for any kind of luxury. As a matter of fact, Coretta worked a little, too, as a child. She hoed and picked cotton, the way so many black children do in Alabama.

There was a one-room schoolhouse for the black children in Heiberger. Coretta walked the five miles to that schoolhouse every morning, and she walked those five miles back home every afternoon. The white children didn't have to walk those miles to their school; they had a bus. Coretta watched them board that bus, followed them as the bus drove by. This was perhaps Coretta's first experience with the so-called "separate but equal" education in the South. She resented it, even as a child and promised herself that one day black and white children would share a bus.

It was in the missionary high school in nearby Marion that Coretta became aware of her special abilities in music. She studied the piano and took voice lessons. When she was graduated in 1945, she went to Antioch, in Yellow Springs, Ohio, intending to pursue a musical career.

She had a scholarship for Antioch, but there wasn't the money at home for a college education. Coretta knew, too, that there wouldn't be the funds she would need for any intensive work in music. The only way to meet that need was to have a job. She decided she would become a teacher and use her salary to forward her studies in music.

The decision, however, had to be changed. Antioch has had a reputation for its progressive education and policies for many years. The area around the college, unfortunately, was not quite as progressive. When Coretta went out to do her practice teaching, she found the doors of the schools closed to her. They did not want any black teachers in their classrooms.

It was, indeed, a terribly unpleasant experience for the young woman. She fought the decisions of the bigoted schools, as she would fight every form of bigotry. This was one battle, however, in her persistent war for equality which she could not win—not just then. She added the schools to her feelings about buses, two areas of inequality to which she would return. Meanwhile, she decided to concentrate on her music.

A fellowship helped her enroll at the New England Conservatory of Music. The fellowship, of course, wasn't enough to live on, and she got a job as a part-time mail order clerk. She arranged to help with a lady's housekeeping, in exchange for a bed and breakfast. There were times when Coretta ate only crackers and peanut butter and some fruit, but she was determined to pursue her education and a musical career.

It was while she was at the Conservatory that she met the young Martin Luther King, Jr., who was doing graduate work in philosophy at Boston University. They lived not too far away from each other and, between classes and studies, they managed to see each other.

They discovered they liked the same things and had the same dreams. Most important, they discovered that they both wanted to fight for those dreams.

They were married June 18, 1953.

In the fall of 1954, Martin Luther King, Jr. was offered the pastorate of a Baptist Church in Montgomery, Alabama; and the young Kings went back South, and to their glory.

It was in the winter of 1955 that Martin Luther King, Jr. inspired and led the Alabama bus boycott. Its aim was to break down the "back of the bus" Jim Crow practice of the bus companies. This was the beginning of the non-violent civil rights crusade which Martin Luther King, Jr. would lead until the day of his death with Coretta King at his side.

She attended every meeting and rally. She was at every important march with her husband. She would give birth to four children during this period: Yolanda Denise in 1955, Martin Luther III in 1957, Dexter Scott in 1961 and Bernice Albertina in 1963. Still, Coretta King was always there in the battle for civil rights. For all her duties as a mother, if her husband could not fulfill an engagement, Coretta King was there to speak for their cause.

In 1956, a bomb was thrown into their house. Fortunately, no one was hurt this time. If she had never known it before, Coretta King knew it then: the life of her husband, her children, her own life, would have to be lived under the ever-present threat of violent death.

The Kings, however, were not to be deterred.

In 1957, the Southern Christian Leadership Conference was organized and Martin Luther King, Jr. was elected its president. The civil rights battle deepened. Black people walked into restaurants which had refused to serve them and kept their seats until they were violently ousted. White and black volunteers moved into the South to open the election polls to black people. The South was in a ferment, and there was violence, but under the guidance of Martin Luther King, Jr., the black people remained non-violent.

In 1960, the Kings moved to Atlanta. Martin Luther King, Jr. shared the pastorate of the Ebenezer Baptist Church with his father. The battle continued from the capital of Georgia.

It was on August 28, 1963 that the largest rally in the history of our nation's capital took place. It was "The March on Washington" for civil rights, and Coretta was there with her husband leading the march.

She was with her husband, too, in Oslo, Norway, on October 14, 1964, when he was awarded the Nobel Peace Prize. She had been to Europe before with her husband in 1959, touring the continent, and Asia as well, in the quest for equality and peace among all peoples.

Nor was Coretta just a companion to this great man. She was an American delegate at the Women's Strike for Peace which met at a disarmament conference in Geneva. She attended countless freedom rallies and sang at Freedom Concerts, collecting much needed funds for the Southern Christian Leadership Conference. She even took the time to teach voice at Atlanta's Morris Brown College.

Martin Luther King, Jr. said, at that famous Washington peace rally, "I had a dream."

The "dream" was only just about beginning to take shape when the assassin's bullet cut short his life in Memphis, the evening of April 4, 1968.

The whole world mourned his death. He was mourned by both black and white who felt the loss of this great leader.

When a leader falls, others must spring up to take his place. There was a great surge to name Coretta King president of the Southern Christian Leadership Conference, and Coretta took her place in the council. She had fought at the side of her husband but she would not take his presidency. She would serve his cause, and her cause, and the cause of her people, as best she could.

It was Coretta King, one of America's endearing heroines, who spoke the last words for Martin Luther King, Jr.

He was a leader in the "Poor People's March on Washington." He had been scheduled as one of its leading speakers.

As she had done so often in the past, Coretta King spoke for her fallen husband.

"Unite and form a solid block of women power," she called out from the Lincoln Memorial in Washington, "to fight the three great evils of racism, poverty and war."

She spoke for her husband. She spoke for herself. This great American woman spoke for all people of good will.

INDEX

Adams, Maude, 110
Addams, Jane, 9, 10-16, 18
Anderson, Marian, 114-18
Anthony, Susan B., 9, 24

Barrymore, Ethel, 110, 113
Barton, Clara, 9, 32-40
Battle Hymn of the Republic, The, 24
Bell, Alexander Graham, 58
Bethune, Mary McLeod, 53-56, 95, 96
Birth Control Review, 67
Blackwell, Elizabeth, 9, 25-31
Block, Anita, 66
Boghetti, Giuseppe, 115
Bourke-White, Margaret, 121-23
Brewster, Mary, 20
Buck, Pearl S., 104-5
Butler, N. M., 16

Carpenter, Mrs. Benjamin, 68
Carson, Rachel, 9, 106-9
Chase, Mary Ellen, 91
Chisholm, Shirley, 95-97
Comstock, Anthony, 65
Corbin, Margaret, 8
Cornell, Katherine, 110-12
Culver, Helen, 15

Dennett, Mary Ware, 66
Dickson, John, 27
Douglass, Frederick, 47
Dragon Seed, 106
Duniway, Abigail, 9

Earhart, Amelia, 78-85
East Wind, West Wind, 104
Edge of the Sea, The, 108
Eisenhower, Dwight D., 77

Family Limitation, 65, 66
Fighting Angel, The, 106
Fiske, Minnie M., 112
Fuller, Sarah, 61, 62

Garfield, James, 39
Good Earth, The, 104, 106
Guest, Mrs. Frederick, 81

Hale, Edward E., 59
Halton, Mary, 68
Hawks, Frank, 79
Hayes, Helen, 111-13
Henry Street Settlement, 21
Higginson, T. W., 46
Horace Mann School for the Deaf, 61
Howe, Julia Ward, 8, 24
Howe, Samuel G., 58
Hull House, 15
Hutchinson, Anne, 8

Ickes, Harold L., 116
International Red Cross, 38

Jacobs, Aletta, 66
Jewett, Sara Orne, 91

Keller, Helen, 57-63
Kennedy, John F., 77

King, Coretta, 128-33
King, Jr., Martin Luther, 128-33

Laney, Lucy, 54
Lincoln, Abraham, 10, 11, 24,
  35, 37, 46
Lindbergh, Charles A., 80-83
Lippman, Walter, 16
Loeb, Mrs. Solomon, 20

Massachusetts Commission for the
  Blind, 62
May, Samuel J., 47
Millay, Edna St. Vincent, 104
Mitchell, Maria, 9, 125-7
Montgomery, James, 46, 47
Mott, Lucretia, 22, 24

National Birth Control League, 66
National Woman Suffrage
  Assoc., 24

O'Keefe, Georgia, 119, 120
Owen, Robert D., 66

Perkins Institute for the Blind, 58
Putnam, George, 82

Reifsnyder, Agnes, 115
Roosevelt, Eleanor, 9, 70-77
Roosevelt, Franklin D., 55, 72-75,
  77, 83
Rucker, General, 36
Rutgers, Johannes, 66

Sanger, Margaret, 64-69
Schiff, Jacob, 20
Sea Around Us, The, 106

Sibelius, Jean, 116
Silent Spring, 108
Smith, Clyde H., 92
Smith, Margaret Chase, 91-95
Snook, Neta, 80
Stanton, Elizabeth Cady, 22, 24
Starr, Ellen, 14
Stieglitz, Alfred, 119
Stillman, Clara, 66
Stone, Hannah, 69
Story of My Life, The, 62
Stowe, Calvin E., 102-4
Stowe, Harriet Beecher, 8, 102-4
Stultz, Bill, 81, 82
Sullivan, Anne M., 59-62

Toscanini, Arturo, 116
Truman, Harry S., 55, 76, 77
Truth, Sojourner, 49-52
Tubman, Harriet, 41-48, 95
Twenty Hours, Forty Minutes, 82

Uncle Tom's Cabin, 8, 104
Wald, Lillian, 17-21
Washington, George, 101
Wharton, Edith, 104
Wheatley, Mrs. John, 79-101
Wheatley, Phillis, 99-102
Wiggin, Kate D., 91
Woman Rebel, 65
World I Live In, The, 63

Yarros, Rachelle, 68
Youth's Companion, 62

Zaharias, Mildred D. (Babe),
  86-90
Zenger, Anna, 8, 99